THE **W**ORD ON

SPIRITUAL WARFARE

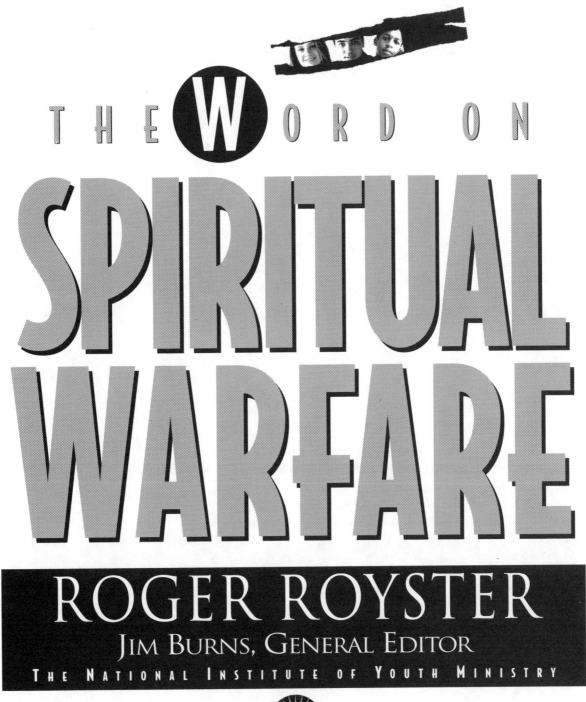

ROGER ROYSTER

JIM BURNS, GENERAL EDITOR

THE NATIONAL INSTITUTE OF YOUTH MINISTRY

Gospel Light

Gospel Light is an evangelical Christian publisher dedicated to serving the local church. We believe God's vision for Gospel Light is to provide church leaders with biblical, user-friendly materials that will help them evangelize, disciple and minister to children, youth and families.

We hope this Gospel Light resource will help you discover biblical truth for your own life and help you minister to youth. God bless you in your work.

For a free catalog of resources from Gospel Light please contact your Christian supplier or call 1-800-4-GOSPEL.

PUBLISHING STAFF

William T. Greig, Publisher
Dr. Elmer L. Towns, Senior Consulting Publisher
Dr. Gary S. Greig, Senior Consulting Editor
Jean Daly, Managing Editor
Pam Weston, Editorial Assistant
Kyle Duncan, Editorial Director
Bayard Taylor, M.Div., Editor, Theological and Biblical Issues
Joey O'Connor, Contributing Writer
Mario Ricketts, Designer

ISBN 0-8307-1724-2
© 1996 Jim Burns
All rights reserved.
Printed in U.S.A.

HOW TO MAKE CLEAN COPIES FROM THIS BOOK

PRAISE FOR YOUTHBUILDERS

Jim Burns knows young people. He also knows how to communicate to them. This study should be in the hands of every youth leader interested in discipling young people.

David Adams, Vice President, Lexington Baptist College

I deeply respect and appreciate the groundwork Jim Burns has prepared for true teenage discernment. YouthBuilders is timeless in the sense that the framework has made it possible to plug into any society, at any point in time, and to proceed to discuss, experience and arrive at sincere moral and Christian conclusions that will lead to growth and life changes. Reaching young people may be more difficult today than ever before, but God's grace is alive and well in Jim Burns and this wonderful curriculum.

Fr. Angelo J. Artemas, Youth Ministry Director, Greek Orthodox Archdiocese of North and South America

I heartily recommend Jim Burns's *YouthBuilders Group Bible Studies* because they are leader-friendly tools that are ready to use in youth groups and Sunday School classes. Jim addresses the tough questions that students are genuinely facing every day and, through his engaging style, challenges young people to make their own decisions to move from their current opinions to God's convictions taught in the Bible. Every youth group will benefit from this excellent curriculum.

Paul Borthwick, Minister of Missions, Grace Chapel

Jim Burns recognizes the fact that small groups are where life change happens. In this study he has captured the essence of that value. Further, Jim has given much thought to shaping this very effective material into a usable tool that serves the parent, leader and student.

Bo Boshers, Executive Director, Student Impact, Willow Creek Community Church

It is about time that someone who knows kids, understands kids and works with kids writes youth curriculum that youth workers, both volunteer and professional, can use. Jim Burns's *YouthBuilders Group Bible Studies* is the curriculum that youth ministry has been waiting a long time for.
Ridge Burns, President,
The Center for Student Missions

There are very few people in the world who know how to communicate life-changing truth effectively to teens. Jim Burns is one of the best. *YouthBuilders Group Bible Studies* puts handles on those skills and makes them available to everyone. These studies are biblically sound, hands-on practical and just plain fun. This one gets a five-star endorsement—which isn't bad since there are only four stars to start with.
Ken Davis, President,
Dynamic Communications

I don't know anyone who knows and understands the needs of the youth worker like Jim Burns. His new curriculum not only reveals his knowledge of youth ministry but also his depth and sensitivity to the Scriptures. *YouthBuilders Group Bible Studies* is solid, easy to use and gets students out of their seats and into the Word. I've been waiting for something like this for a long time!
Doug Fields, Pastor of High School,
Saddleback Valley Community Church

Jim Burns has a way of being creative without being "hokey." *YouthBuilders Group Bible Studies* takes the age-old model of curriculum and gives it a new look with tools such as the Bible *Tuck-In*™ and Parent Page. Give this new resource a try and you'll see that Jim shoots straightforward on tough issues. The *YouthBuilders* series is great for leading small-group discussions as well as teaching a large class of junior high or high school students. The Parent Page will help you get support from your parents in that they will understand the topics you

are dealing with in your group. Put Jim's years of experience to work for you by equipping yourself with this quality material.
Curt Gibson, Pastor to Junior High,
First Church of the Nazarene of Pasadena

Once again, Jim Burns has managed to handle very timely issues with just the right touch. His *YouthBuilders Group Bible Studies* succeeds in teaching solid biblical values without being stuffy or preachy. The format is user-friendly, designed to stimulate high involvement and deep discussion. Especially impressive is the Parent Page, a long overdue tool to help parents become part of the Christian education loop. I look forward to using it with my kids!
David M. Hughes, Pastor,
First Baptist Church, Winston-Salem

What do you get when you combine a deep love for teens, over 20 years' experience in youth ministry and an excellent writer? You get Jim Burns's *YouthBuilders* series! This stuff has absolutely hit the nail on the head. Quality Sunday School and small-group material is tough to come by these days, but Jim has put every ounce of creativity he has into these books.
Greg Johnson, author of *Getting Ready for the Guy/Girl Thing* and *Keeping Your Cool While Sharing Your Faith*

Jim Burns has a gift, the gift of combining the relational and theological dynamics of our faith in a graceful, relevant and easy-to-chew-and-swallow way. *YouthBuilders Group Bible Studies* is a hit, not only for teens but for teachers.
Gregg Johnson, National Youth Director,
International Church of the Foursquare Gospel

The practicing youth worker always needs more ammunition. Here is a whole book full of practical, usable resources for those facing kids face-to-face. *YouthBuilders Group Bible Studies* will get that blank stare off the faces of kids in your youth meeting!
Jay Kesler, President, Taylor University

I couldn't be more excited about the *YouthBuilders Group Bible Studies.* It couldn't have arrived at a more needed time. Spiritually we approach the future engaged in war with young people taking direct hits from the devil. This series will practically help teens who feel partially equipped to "put on the whole armor of God."
Mike MacIntosh, Pastor,
Horizon Christian Fellowship

In *YouthBuilders Group Bible Studies,* Jim Burns pulls together the key ingredients for an effective curriculum series. Jim captures the combination of teen involvement and a solid biblical perspective, with topics that are relevant and straightforward. This series will be a valuable tool in the local church.
Dennis "Tiger" McLuen, Executive Director,
Youth Leadership

My ministry takes me to the lost kids in our nation's cities where youth games and activities are often irrelevant and plain Bible knowledge for the sake of learning is unattractive. Young people need the information necessary to make wise decisions related to everyday problems. *YouthBuilders* will help many young people integrate their faith into everyday life, which after all is our goal as youth workers.
Miles McPherson, President, Project Intercept

Jim Burns's passion for teens, youth workers and parents of teens is evident in the *YouthBuilders Group Bible Studies.* He has a gift of presenting biblical truths on a

level teens will fully understand, and youth workers and parents can easily communicate.
Al Menconi, President, Al Menconi Ministries

Youth ministry curriculum is often directed to only one spoke of the wheel of youth ministry—the adolescent. Not so with this material! Jim has enlarged the education circle, including information for the adolescent, the parent and the youth worker. *YouthBuilders Group Bible Studies* is youth and family ministry-oriented material at its best.
Helen Musick, Instructor of Youth Ministry,
Asbury Seminary

Finally, a Bible study that has it all! It's action-packed, practical and biblical; but that's only the beginning. *YouthBuilders* involves students in the Scriptures. It's relational, interactive and leads kids toward lifestyle changes. The unique aspect is a page for parents, something that's usually missing from adolescent curriculum. Jim Burns has outdone himself. This isn't a home run—it's a grand slam!
Dr. David Olshine, Director of Youth Ministries,
Columbia International University

Here is a thoughtful and relevant curriculum designed to meet the needs of youth workers, parents and students. It's creative, interactive and biblical—and with Jim Burns's name on it, you know you're getting a quality resource.
Laurie Polich, Youth Director,
First Presbyterian Church of Berkeley

In 10 years of youth ministry I've never used a curriculum because I've never found anything that actively involves students in the learning process, speaks to young people where they are and challenges them with biblical truth—I'll use this! *YouthBuilders Group Bible Studies* is a complete curriculum that is helpful to parents, youth leaders and, most importantly, today's youth.

Glenn Schroeder, Youth and Young Adult Ministries, Vineyard Christian Fellowship, Anaheim

This new material by Jim Burns represents a vitality in curriculum and, I believe, a more mature and faithful direction. *YouthBuilders Group Bible Studies* challenges youth by teaching them how to make decisions rather than telling them what decisions to make. Each session offers teaching concepts, presents options and asks for a decision. I believe it's healthy, the way Christ taught and represents the abilities, personhood and faithfulness of youth. I give it an A+!

J. David Stone, President, Stone & Associates

Jim Burns has done it again! This is a practical, timely and reality-based resource for equipping teens to live life in the fast-paced, pressure-packed adolescent world of the '90s. A very refreshing creative oasis in the curriculum desert!

Rich Van Pelt, President, Alongside Ministries

YouthBuilders Group Bible Studies is a tremendous new set of resources for reaching students. Jim has his finger on the pulse of youth today. He understands their mind-sets, and has prepared these studies in a way that will capture their attention and lead to greater maturity in Christ. I heartily recommend these studies.

Rick Warren, Senior Pastor, Saddleback Valley Community Church

CONTENTS

THANKS AND THANKS AGAIN!

I must begin by thanking Kim, my wife, friend, playmate and biggest fan. I would not be who I am, where I am today if it wasn't for your influence on my life. You have been incredibly supportive during this whole process, even while being pregnant. Your words ring loud in my ears, "Don't lose sight of your dreams." Thank You! I love you!

Thank you as well to Jim Burns, my mentor and friend. You have been a catalyst in my life in many ways. Specifically you have given me the opportunity to make a personal dream come true in the writing of this project.

Thank you to my Mom and Dad who have loved and loved and loved some more. Thanks for leading me to a place where I could find God. Thanks for being GREAT parents.

Thanks to my family: Steve, Jane, Stefany, Emily, Andy, Dave and Lora. You're an awesome family.

Thanks to my fellow staff members at NIYM in San Clemente: Dean Bruns, Luchi Bierbower, Laurie Pilz, Doug Webster, Larry Acosta, Jill Corey and Gary Lenhardt. People need to feel like they belong somewhere with somebody. You guys do that for me. Thank you for your support.

Thank you to Jean Daly and Gospel Light for the opportunity to do this project.

Thanks to the Roger Royster Adventure Club, my supporters. Your support of me in ministry has made a statement to me about the body of Christ that I can't find words to express. God has used you greatly in my life. Thank You!

Father God, thank You for giving me bread not rocks. I love You.

DEDICATION

To Hayden James Royster,

I have yet to know the gift you will be to me, but within four days of writing these words you will be born. I will hold you for the first time and the adventure will begin. I have asked God to give you a heart that longs to restore the intimacy you share with Him now. It's my hope to be there the day you welcome Him back into your life.

I love you, Son.

YOUTHBUILDERS GROUP BIBLE STUDIES

It's Relational—Students learn best when they talk—not when you talk. There is always a get acquainted section in the Warm Up. All the experiences are based on building community in your group.

It's Biblical—With no apologies, this series in unashamedly Christian. Every session has a practical, relevant Bible study.

It's Experiential—Studies show that young people retain up to 85 percent of the material when they are *involved* in action-oriented, experiential learning. The sessions use role-plays, discussion starters, case studies, graphs and other experiential, educational methods. *We believe it's a sin to bore a young person with the gospel.*

It's Interactive—This study is geared to get students feeling comfortable with sharing ideas and interacting with peers and leaders.

It's Easy to Follow—The sessions have been prepared by Jim Burns to allow the leader to pick up the material and use it. There is little preparation time on your part. Jim did the work for you.

It's Adaptable—You can pick and choose from several topics or go straight through the material as a whole study.

It's Age Appropriate—In the "Team Effort" section, one group experience relates best to junior high students while the other works better with high school students. Look at both to determine which option is best for your group.

It's Parent Oriented—The Parent Page helps you to do youth ministry at its finest. Christian education should take place in the home as well as in the church. The Parent Page is your chance to come alongside the parents and help them have a good discussion with their kids.

It's Proven—This material was not written by someone in an ivory tower. It was written for young people and has already been used with them. They love it.

HOW TO USE THIS STUDY

The 12 sessions are divided into three stand-alone units. Each unit has four sessions. You may choose to teach all 12 sessions consecutively. Or you may use only one unit. Or you may present individual sessions. You know your group best so you choose.

Each of the 12 sessions is divided into five sections.

Warm Up—Young people will stay in your youth group if they feel comfortable and make friends in the group. This section is designed for you and the students to get to know each other better. These activities are filled with history-giving and affirming questions and experiences.

Team Effort—Following the model of Jesus, the Master Teacher, these activities engage young people in the session. Stories, group situations, surveys and more bring the session to the students. There is an option for junior high/middle school students and one for high school students.

In the Word—Most young people are biblically illiterate. These Bible studies present the Word of God and encourage students to see the relevance of the Scriptures to their lives.

Things to Think About—Young people need the opportunity to really think through the issues at hand. These discussion starters get students talking about the subject and interacting on important issues.

Parent Page—A youth worker can only do so much. Reproduce this page and get it into the hands of parents. This tool allows quality parent/teen communication that really brings the session home.

THE BIBLE *TUCK-IN*™

It's a tear-out sheet you fold and place in your Bible, containing the essentials you'll need for teaching your group.

HERE'S HOW TO USE IT:

To prepare for the session, first study the session. Tear out the Bible *Tuck-In*™ and personalize it by making notes. Fold the Bible *Tuck-In*™ in half on the dotted line. Slip it into your Bible for easy reference throughout the session. The Key Verse, Biblical Basis and Big Idea at the beginning of the Bible *Tuck-In*™ will help you keep the session on track. With the Bible *Tuck-In*™ your students will see that your teaching comes from the Bible and won't be distracted by a leader's guide.

GOD IS ON OUR SIDE

LEADER'S PEP TALK

I must have been in the fourth grade the day my dad saved my life. For weeks I had been threatened, harassed and frightened by a kid from my neighborhood elementary school. The only reason I can find to justify this kid's behavior toward me was that I was the only kid in our class that was smaller than he was. I guess that made me an obvious target for a preteen trying to affirm his growing manhood.

Across the street from my own home was where the fist hit the garage door, as they say. The fist was actually my fist missing its intended target in a poor attempt at defending my honor. Like two bad dancers, we did what many untrained preteen fighters do, fell to the ground rolling across the cement in an attempt to get a punch in here or there. Suddenly the action stopped as the figure of a man quickly pulled my sparring partner from my clutches. It was my dad. Where did he come from?

It was at that moment I saw my dad do something I thought I would never see. He held this kid high off the ground by his collar, then placed him down just inches from his own feet. Looking him in the eye, he gave a huge karate-style "Hey!" into his face. This yell was so shocking that it scared the fluids right out of this kid's body.

My dad then stepped between my opponent and me and said, "I understand you have been threatening my son, is this true?" The kid squeaked out a yes. "Well the truth is," my dad said, "when you mess with a child of mine, you mess with me. Now get out of here and don't bother us again." I have never seen a kid with wet pants run any faster.

> "What, then, shall we say in response to this? If God is for us, who can be
>
> against us? He who did not spare his own Son, but gave him up for us all—how
>
> will he not also, along with him, graciously give us all things?" (Romans 8:31,32)

As you lead your students through this section, you will no doubt be reminded of how much the heavenly Father does to protect His children. Help your students discover how liberating, freeing and especially healing the information in this section can be.

The truth is that we as leaders need to be intimately acquainted with our heavenly Father who waits to give us loaves of bread, not bags of rocks (see Matthew 7:9). As you work through this section together, it is my prayer for you that the security of a life-changing Christ would become the source of strength you need to stand against the enemy.

SALVATION:
A GIFT FROM GOD

 **EY VERSES**

"For it is by grace you have been saved, through faith—and this not from yourselves, it is the gift of God—not by works, so that no one can boast." Ephesians 2:8,9

B IBLICAL BASIS

Psalm 116:5,6;
Romans 5:12; 8:38,39;
1 Corinthians 15:21,22;
Ephesians 2:1-8,10; 5:1-6;
1 John 4:8

T HE BIG IDEA

The first step in standing our ground against the enemy is to secure our salvation through Christ's *life-giving* love.

 **IMS OF THIS SESSION**

During this session you will guide students to:

• Examine the three Bs of Christ's life-giving love;
• Discover how to be made alive by God's love and grace;
• Implement a life of salvation in Christ Jesus.

 **ARM UP**

WHY, WHEN AND HOW—

A discussion about the impact of Christ's life-changing love on students' lives.

 **EAM EFFORT— JUNIOR HIGH/ MIDDLE SCHOOL**

PENNY HUNT—

A game to illustrate the parable of the lost coin.

T EAM EFFORT— HIGH SCHOOL

ACT IT OUT—

Three role-playing situations about salvation.

 **N THE WORD**

THE THREE BS OF A SECURE SALVATION—

A Bible study on the meaning of salvation to believers' lives.

T HINGS TO THINK ABOUT (OPTIONAL)

Questions to get students thinking and talking about the meaning of being spiritually lost.

P ARENT PAGE

A tool to get the session into the home and allow parents and young people to discuss a modern-day parable about being saved.

**SALVATION:
A GIFT FROM GOD**

LEADER'S DEVOTIONAL

"The Lord is gracious and righteous; our God is full of compassion. The Lord protects the simplehearted; when I was in great need, he saved me" (Psalm 116:5,6).

You are a target. As a youth worker involved with the critical task of shaping, nurturing and developing the lives of young people, you are a target for spiritual attack. Now before you get the willies, don't think I'm one who believes that the devil lurks behind every 7-11 Slurpee machine or that every misfortune or accident is caused by the devil himself. No, Satan is smoother than that. He is slick, calculated, deliberate. His schemes are designed to wreak the most havoc, impacting as many lives as possible. That's why you and every person involved in active ministry are a target for his demonic work in this world. If you were a naval commander, would you go after individual planes or the aircraft carrier itself? Youth workers are aircraft carriers deploying young Christians all over the world in various missions.

Like a roaring lion pursuing its prey, Satan only pursues living, active followers of Christ—people who are truly making a difference in this world for the kingdom of God. Lions don't stalk dead or diseased prey. While serving young people and their families, we would be ignorant and foolish to ignore God's perspective on spiritual warfare. That's why it's so important to develop a clear and secure perspective on salvation. You and I are first of all children of God who are saved by His love and grace and heirs of His kingdom. We need not be scared, bleating sheep surrounded by ravenous wolves because He has promised to be our Protector.

Yes, we are in a spiritual battle and the targets of any weapon Satan will use to destroy our relationships with God, but we fight an enemy who has limited power. Satan has limited abilities, limited resources and best of all, limited time.

Discovering your security in Christ and helping students to discover theirs is a wonderful gift to impart to them. When you are secure in Christ, you are in a position to firmly stand your ground against the enemy. You have all of God's unlimited firepower to fight off Satan's attacks. The reason for your spiritual battle is because of God's gift of salvation to you. So, it is from a position of salvation that your battles are fought. When you are entrenched in your security in Christ, you are an indestructible target. These lessons will arm you with everything you need from the Holy Spirit and the power of God's Word to stand your ground. (Written by Joey O'Connor.)

**"If salvation could be attained only by working hard, then surely horses and donkeys would be in heaven."
—Martin Luther**

SALVATION: A GIFT FROM GOD

KEY VERSES

"For it is by grace you have been saved, through faith—and this not from yourselves, it is the gift of God—not by works, so that no one can boast." Ephesians 2:8,9

BIBLICAL BASIS

Psalm 116:5,6; Romans 5:12; 8:38,39; 1 Corinthians 15:21,22; Ephesians 2:1-8,10; 5:1-6; 1 John 4:8

THE BIG IDEA

The first step in standing our ground against the enemy is to secure our salvation through Christ's life-giving love.

WARM UP (5-10 MINUTES)

WHY, WHEN AND HOW

- Give each student a copy of "Why, When and How" on page 19 and a pen or pencil.
- Give the students two minutes to answer the questions by themselves.
- Discuss the questions with the whole group.
- Optional: Display a copy using an overhead and discuss the questions with the whole group.

1. What is salvation and why is it such an important factor in life?

2. When in your life have you experienced the effects of Christ's life-changing love? How did it happen?

3. Has Christ made a difference in your life? In what ways?

--- Fold ---

2. Read Ephesians 2:4,5. Why did God make us alive with Christ even though we were dead in our sin?

3. First John 4:8 says that if we do not love, we do not .... because ....

4. What does Ephesians 2:8 tell us we must have to be saved by love?

5. Where does Ephesians 2:4-8 say the love, faith and grace we need for our salvation comes from?

BROUGHT TO A LIFE OF GOOD WORKS

1. Ephesians 2:10 says we are brought to a love-filled life for a reason. What is that reason?

2. Whose example of a life of good works does Ephesians 5:1,2 tell us we can follow?

3. How does this verse say we can imitate God?

SO WHAT?

Romans 8:38,39 says "For I am convinced that neither death nor life, neither angels nor demons, neither the present nor any powers, neither height nor depth, nor anything else in all creation, will be able to separate us from the love of God that is in Christ Jesus our Lord."

You are secure in your salvation if you have allowed God's life-giving love into your life. How does it make you feel knowing that nothing can separate you from God's love?

THINGS TO THINK ABOUT (OPTIONAL)

- Use the questions on page 23 after or as part of "In the Word."

1. What is the first thing that comes to your mind when you hear the word "lost"?

2. What do you think it means when a person who does not know Christ is called lost?

3. Before you experienced Christ's salvation, in what ways were you lost?

PARENT PAGE

- Distribute page to parents.

Team Effort—Junior High/Middle School (15-20 Minutes)

Penny Hunt

- Beforehand hide 100 pennies throughout the room, or in a designated area outside. Don't make the hiding places too difficult.
- Divide the students into two groups. Designate one group as the "Dark Team" and one group as the "Light Team."
- Give each group a "piggy bank" or a paper cup.
- Tell the students that each hidden penny represents a person who is lost and needs to be found and they are to find as many "lost pennies" as they can in five minutes.
- When five minutes is up, gather the students together. Have them count the pennies they have collected. The game is won by the team that finds the most pennies.
- Discuss the following questions:
  1. In order to win the game what did your team have to do?
  2. If the pennies really did represent people in the world who do not have a relationship with Jesus, what has to happen before they can have a personal relationship with Him?
  3. What is the significance of the teams being named the "Dark Team" and the "Light Team? Which team do we want to be on? Why?
  4. What are the eternal issues involved in our salvation?

Team Effort—High School (15-20 Minutes)

Act It Out

- Make copies of "Act It Out" on page 20 and cut apart the three situations.
- Divide students into three groups.
- Give each group copies of one of the following "Act It Out" situations.
- Give students about seven minutes to read and discuss their group's situation.
- After the groups have discussed their situation, have them select two members to role-play the situation before the whole group.
- After all of the role-plays have been presented, discuss the last two questions with the whole group.

Act It Out One (A Girl And A Guy Needed)
Discuss the following questions:
1. Sharon needs to understand what salvation means and how it will change her life. How would you explain this to her?
2. What did you need to know about Christ's salvation before choosing to give your life to Him?
Now choose two members of your group to act out what your group has discussed. Ready? Act it out!

Act It Out Two (Two Girls Needed)
Discuss the following questions:
1. How would you explain to Lisa about the salvation that believers receive from Christ?
2. What did you need to know about Christ's salvation before choosing to give your life to Him?
Now choose two members of your group to act out what your group has discussed. Ready? Act it out!

Fold

Act It Out Three (Two Guys Needed)
Discuss the following questions:
1. What are the important concepts a person needs to understand in order to experience salvation in Christ?
2. What did you need to know about Christ's salvation before choosing to give your life to Him?
Now choose two members of your group to act out what your group has discussed. Ready? Act it out!

- Discussion questions:
1. What are some things about salvation that you have a hard time understanding?
2. When and how did you come to understand the salvation you received from Christ? (Note to leader: Briefly share your own experience to encourage students to share.)

In The Word (25-30 Minutes)

- Divide students into groups of three or four.
- Give each student a copy of "In the Word" on pages 21-23 and a pen or pencil, or display a copy using an overhead projector.
- Have students complete the Bible study.

Brought From Death To Life
1. What does Ephesians 2:1 say is the result of living a life of sin?

2. Look up Romans 5:12 and I Corinthians 15:21,22. Through whom did we inherit spiritual death and how did it happen?

3. Who and what does Ephesians 2:2 say is the result of living a life of sin?

4. What does it mean to you that before receiving salvation from Christ, you followed the ways of the enemy?

5. Ephesians 5:3-6 lists some words that describe behaviors common to us when we live a life of sin. The column headings below are those words and statements. Under each heading list things that people do today that are a sin.

Sexual Immorality	Impurity
Greed	
Foolish Talk	
Coarse Joking	

Brought Alive By God's Love And Grace
1. A sin-filled life has been defined as "a life lived separated from God's life-giving love." How do the people you know try to meet their need for that lost love in their lives?

The Three Bs Of A Secure Salvation

WARM UP

WHY, WHEN AND HOW

1. What is salvation and why is it such an important factor in life?

....

....

....

2. When in your life have you experienced the effects of Christ's life-changing love? How did it happen?

....

....

....

3. Has Christ made a difference in your life? In what ways?

....

....

....

SALVATION:
A GIFT FROM GOD

GOD IS ON OUR SIDE

TEAM EFFORT

ACT IT OUT

Act It Out One (a girl and a guy needed)

Joe has been a Christian for five years and has just returned from camp where he finally understood what it means to experience salvation through Christ. Joe is sitting reading his Bible when Sharon walks up and sits down next to him.

Sharon looks at Joe and says, "Joe, my life is a mess. I feel so lost. I wish I had something that would save me from my circumstances and change my life forever."

Discuss the following questions:

1. Sharon needs to understand what salvation means and how it will change her life. How would you explain this to her?
2. What did you need to know about Christ's salvation before choosing to give your life to Him?

Now choose two members of your group to act out what your group has discussed. Ready? Act it out!

Act It Out Two (two girls needed)

Lisa has quite a reputation around school for being really worldly. Her parents are pretty wealthy. Lisa has a nice car, nice clothes and plenty of spending money.

One day in a conversation with Julie, Lisa makes the comment that she is so unhappy with her life. Julie and Lisa know each other, but they have never been good friends. They first met in fifth grade Sunday School back when Lisa and her family went to church. Julie knows Lisa needs to know Jesus and to understand what it means to be saved by Him.

Discuss the following questions:

1. How would you explain to Lisa about the salvation that believers receive from Christ?
2. What did you need to know about Christ's salvation before choosing to give your life to Him?

Now choose two members of your group to act out what your group has discussed. Ready? Act it out!

Act It Out Three (two guys needed)

Bill is the shortstop on his school's baseball team. All the players really look up to him. The baseball coach calls him into his office one day and asks Bill if he would be willing to share a team devotional and pray for the team before each game. Bill didn't even know the coach knew he was a Christian. Bill and the coach are having a conversation about what the team needs to know about salvation.

Discuss the following questions:

1. What are the important concepts a person needs to understand in order to experience salvation in Christ?
2. What did you need to know about Christ's salvation before choosing to give your life to Him?

Now choose two members of your group to act out what your group has discussed. Ready? Act it out!

IN THE WORD

THE THREE Bs OF A SECURE SALVATION

Brought from Death to Life

1. What does Ephesians 2:1 say is the result of living a life of sin?

   ....

   ....

2. Look up Romans 5:12 and 1 Corinthians 15:21,22. Through whom did we inherit spiritual death and how did it happen?

   ....

   ....

3. Who and what does Ephesians 2:2 say we were following before accepting salvation in Christ?

   ....

   ....

4. What does it mean to you that before receiving salvation from Christ, you followed the ways of the enemy?

   ....

   ....

5. Ephesians 5:3-6 lists some words that describe behaviors common to us when we live a life of sin. The column headings below are those words and statements. Under each heading list things that people do today that are sin.

Sexual Immorality	Impurity
Greed	**Obscenity**
Foolish Talk	**Disobedience**

**SALVATION:
A GIFT FROM GOD**

Coarse Joking

Deception

....

....

Brought Alive by God's Love and Grace

1. A sin-filled life has been defined as "a life lived separated from God's life-giving love." How do the people you know try to meet their need for that lost love in their lives?

....

....

2. Read Ephesians 2:4,5. Why did God make us alive with Christ even though we were dead in our sin?

....

....

3. First John 4:8 says that if we do not love, we do not .... because

....

4. What does Ephesians 2:8 tell us we must have to be saved by love?

....

....

....

5. Where does Ephesians 2:4-8 say the love, faith and grace we need for our salvation comes from?

....

....

Brought to a Life of Good Works

1. Ephesians 2:10 says we are brought to a love-filled life for a reason. What is that reason?

....

....

2. Whose example of a life of good works does Ephesians 5:1,2 tell us we can follow?

....

....

3. How does this verse say we can imitate God?

....

....

SO WHAT?

Romans 8:38,39 says "For I am convinced that neither death nor life, neither angels nor demons, neither the present nor the future, nor any powers, neither height nor depth, nor anything else in all creation, will be able to separate us from the love of God that is in Christ Jesus our Lord."

You are secure in your salvation if you have allowed God's life-giving love into your life. How does it make you feel knowing that nothing can separate you from God's love?

....

....

....

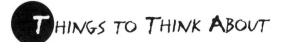 HINGS TO THINK ABOUT

1. What is the first thing that comes to your mind when you hear the word "lost"?

....

....

....

2. What do you think it means when a person who does not know Christ is called lost?

....

....

....

3. Before you experienced Christ's salvation, in what ways were you lost?

....

....

....

**SALVATION:
A GIFT FROM GOD**

PARENT PAGE

SAVED

A few years ago two men were canoeing down the Colorado River. At one point as they were leaving a dock, they accidentally maneuvered their canoe sideways in the current and capsized their canoe. One of the men decided he was strong enough to hold the canoe, swim to the side of the river and save all of their camping equipment.

The truth about the man's strength quickly became evident as the rushing current of the river pulled him, their belongings and the canoe back against the dock and down to the bottom of the river. The man found himself ten feet below the surface pinned between the canoe and the dock pilings by the current.

On the surface the dock attendant frantically rushed around looking for a way to keep this man from drowning. Suddenly, when it seemed all hope of being saved was lost, the man below the surface saw a thin, green garden hose being lowered from above. He grabbed it and began to breathe through the hose until help could come to set him free. Within thirty minutes divers joined him below the surface to help set him free. The divers were able to free him from the place in which he was trapped and in so doing they saved his life.

1. What would you have done if you were the dock attendant?

2. If you were the man who was stuck, what would you have been thinking and feeling?

3. What do you think your first words would have been when the divers brought you to the surface?

4. Spiritually we find ourselves trapped in a similar circumstance in need of being rescued. What does Ephesians 2:1-3 say is the cause for our being trapped?

5. What does Ephesians 2:4 say saves us?

6. When we *are* saved, Ephesians 2:5 says we are...

7. Share with each other any details of your own experience that brought you to a relationship with Christ. Pray together thanking God for the salvation He offers to each of us.

Session 1 "Salvation: A Gift from God"
Date

TRANSFORMATION:
CHRIST CAME TO CHANGE LIVES COMPLETELY

EY VERSES

"Dear friends, let us love one another, for love comes from God. Everyone who loves has been born of God and knows God. Whoever does not love does not know God, because God is love." 1 John 4:7,8

BIBLICAL BASIS

Psalm 16:8,9;
Romans 8:1,2,15; 12:1,2;
2 Corinthians 5:17;
Ephesians 4:22-24;
Colossians 1:21,22;
1 John 4:7,8

THE BIG IDEA

Our lives are changed completely when we expose ourselves to the power of God's love.

AIMS OF THIS SESSION

During this session you will guide students to:
• Examine the power of God's love;
• Discover love's transforming power;
• Implement new actions in the key areas of our lives.

ARM UP

CHANGEABLES—

A game to discover the number of things that can change.

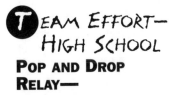EAM EFFORT— JUNIOR HIGH/ MIDDLE SCHOOL

CHANGED FOR LIFE—

Students list the changes that salvation brings to a believer's life.

TEAM EFFORT— HIGH SCHOOL

POP AND DROP RELAY—

A game illustrating how a life changes after salvation.

N THE WORD

A LIFE-CHANGING LOVE—

A Bible study on how Christ changes a life surrendered to Him.

HINGS TO THINK ABOUT (OPTIONAL)

Questions to get students thinking and talking about how to make changes in their own lives.

ARENT PAGE

A tool to get the session into the home and allow parents and students to share how each of them has changed both physically and spiritually.

TRANSFORMATION:
CHRIST CAME TO
CHANGE LIVES
COMPLETELY

LEADER'S DEVOTIONAL

"I have set the Lord always before me. Because he is at my right hand, I will not be shaken. Therefore my heart is glad and my tongue rejoices" (Psalm 16:8,9).

Transformation...I love that word. It is bold, powerful, dynamic. Transformation digs into the very soul of every person's longing for something new—a change, a new beginning. If it wasn't for Christ's power to transform our lives, we'd be living a completely lost, hopeless existence. Transformation is something you and I need on a daily basis.

As a new Christian at sixteen years of age, I often viewed transformation from an external perspective. I didn't drink or do drugs anymore. I changed my music. My vocabulary lost a few colorful adjectives. I treated girls and my friends better than I did before I became a Christian. I know I definitely experienced an inner transformation in Christ which affected my outer world, but I often measured transformation by my external actions. Transformation was based on what I did and not always who I was in Christ.

Unfortunately, in today's Christian world transformation is often viewed by external actions as well. Transformation is touted as a fixed event—a one-time prayer—an instant change from a long life of sin and rebellion against God. When we are born into our new position in Christ that inner transformation often takes a back seat to the importance some people place on the external change in actions. When our spirituality is measured by what we do or don't do, it's easy to track our transformation by our performance. That's what I consider to be a very adolescent view of faith and transformation. It's kind of like expecting a report card from God.

What worked as a teenager won't serve us very well as adults, and that's the challenge I lay before you as you seek daily transformation by the inner life in the Spirit. When I became a Christian, changing the outside was relatively easy, but now as an adult I know the Holy Spirit wants to get into the really tough stuff way down inside of me—serious matters of my heart like my will, pride, desires, thoughts, character, obedience and submission. These are the dark attics of our soul where Christ wants to crawl around for a while with His flashlight. It is the difference between a check-up and major surgery with the Master Physician. It's the kind of transformation I probably couldn't have handled as a sixteen-year-old.

As an adult youth worker, what inner transformation issues does God want you to hand over to Him? Is your faith like many of the adolescents you work with or does it reflect the Holy Spirit's presence at this point in your adult journey of faith? Why such heavy questions you ask? Before we begin teaching and talking to young people about transformation, it's critical to know what kind of transformation we're talking about: external or internal? One leads to the other, one doesn't. There's a critical difference. (Written by Joey O'Connor.)

"After being born again a man experiences peace, but it is a militant peace, a peace maintained at the point of war."
—Oswald Chambers

TRANSFORMATION: CHRIST CAME TO CHANGE LIVES COMPLETELY

KEY VERSES

"Dear friends, let us love one another, for love comes from God. Everyone who loves has been born of God and knows God. Whoever does not love does not know God, because God is love." 1 John 4:7,8

BIBLICAL BASIS

Psalm 16:8,9; Romans 8:1,2,15; 12:1,2; 2 Corinthians 5:17; Ephesians 4:22-24; Colossians 1:21,22; 1 John 4:7,8

THE BIG IDEA

Our lives are changed completely when we expose ourselves to the power of God's love.

WARM UP (5-10 MINUTES)

CHANGEABLES

• Divide students into four teams.

• Give each group a piece of paper and a pen or pencil.

• Tell students that when you say go they will have two minutes to list as many things that they can think of that change somehow (i.e. a caterpillar to a butterfly, ice to water, etc.). "Be creative. Go!"

• When time is up, have the teams count the items on their list. The winning team must read their list.

• Discuss the following questions:

1. How are the changes that a caterpillar goes through similar to the changes a person goes through when they come to know Christ?

2. What are some changes that have happened in your life since you came to know Christ?

Fold

---

4. Take a look at the people in your group. Identify one way you have seen each other changed because of God's love.

SO WHAT?

Christ came to change our lives completely. He desires to leave no area untouched. Evaluate yourself in the areas of change listed below to see how much you've changed since Christ came into your life.

Take a couple of minutes alone right now to consider the following areas of your life. How has knowing Christ changed you? If you haven't really changed in that area yet, consider in what way you can begin to reflect God's life-changing love in your life.

Time:

Values:

Language:

Jokes:

Friends:

Enemies:

Music:

Opposite Sex:

Dating:

Parents:

School:

Church:

Attitudes:

Prayerfully consider one area in which you know you need to change and write down one step you will take in this area in the next week.

In your small group pray for one another concerning the area each of you has chosen to work on.

THINGS TO THINK ABOUT (OPTIONAL)

• Use the questions on page 32 after or as part of "In the Word."

1. What are the biggest changes you have made in your life this past year?

2. What are two areas of change you can work on this next year?

3. What are some specific action steps you can begin to practice today that will help those changes occur?

PARENT PAGE

• Distribute page to parents.

CHANGED FOR LIFE

- Divide students into groups of three or four.
- Give each group a copy of "Changed for Life" on page 29 and a pen or pencil, or display a copy on an overhead projector and give each group blank paper and a pen or pencil.
- Tell them to read the story and list all of the changes that they can think of.
- After about seven to ten minutes, have the groups share their lists.

Now that Derrick is a growing Christian, what are some changes he can expect to take place in his life?

1.
2.
3.
4.
5.
6.
7.
8.
9.
10.

What are two specific changes that took place in your life after you became a Christian?

....

POP AND DROP RELAY

The object of the game is to completely empty the bowl of popped popcorn first by eating it.

- Divide the students into teams of at least five or six.
- Materials Needed:

Popcorn

Air poppers for as many teams as you may have

One large bowl (equal in size) per team

One chair per team

One person as a catcher

One counter per team (not a member of the team)

- Directions: With each team using a hot-air popper with an identical measurement of unpopped kernels in each popper, begin the game by saying "Ready? Pop." As each popper finishes popping all the kernels into a bowl, each team member one by one will carry one handful of popped popcorn to their fellow team member (the catcher) who is lying in the drop zone across the room. This catcher will lay on his or her back with hands at his or her sides and his or her mouth open in the receiving position. The student with the handful of popcorn (the dropper) will step onto the chair that is placed at the head of the catcher in the drop zone. The dropper will drop the popped kernels one at a time into the mouth of the catcher until the dropper's handful is gone and the popcorn is

eaten. The winning team is the team that empties its bowl first and drops the most kernels successfully into the mouth of the catcher.

- Discuss the following questions:

1. In this game how did a team win?

2. When popcorn kernels pop, they change from one form to another. When we invite Christ into our lives, we change from one form to another. In what way have you seen this happen in someone's life?

3. The popped kernels are like specific changes Christ makes in our lives when He comes in. What are two changes you're experiencing in your life that you can see will help others to know Christ better?

A LIFE-CHANGING LOVE

- Divide students into groups of three or four.
- Give each student a copy of "In the Word" on pages 30-31 and a pen or pencil, or display a copy using an overhead projector.
- Have students complete the Bible study.

1. **Why is it hard for people to change?**

....

2. **The Bible tells us that Christ came to change peoples' lives. What changes do these verses say take place because of Christ's love in our lives?**

Romans 8:1,2

Romans 8:15

Romans 12:1,2

2 Corinthians 5:17

Ephesians 4:23,24

Colossians 1:21,22

3. **First John 4:7,8 describes in three stages how change takes place in our lives. Fill in the blanks.**

Stage One:

"*Dear Friends, let us love one another for* ..."

When did you first begin to feel God's love in your life?

....

Stage Two:

"*Everyone who loves* ..."

What is a sign that someone has become a Christian?

....

Stage Three:

"*...has been born of God* ..."

What is the result of being loved by God?

....

TEAM EFFORT

CHANGED FOR LIFE

Derrick is thirteen years old and has grown up in a non-Christian family. Derrick has recently invited Christ into his life because he is ready for some changes. Derrick's friends have not been the best influences on his life and because of that he has been getting into a lot of trouble at school and home. His language and social activities reflect what Derrick's life has been like until now.

Now that Derrick is a growing Christian, what are some changes he can expect to take place in his life?

1. ....
2. ....
3. ....
4. ....
5. ....
6. ....
7. ....
8. ....
9. ....
10. ....

What are two specific changes that took place in your life after you became a Christian?

....

....

**TRANSFORMATION:
CHRIST CAME TO
CHANGE LIVES
COMPLETELY**

 **IN THE WORD**

A LIFE-CHANGING LOVE

1. Why is it hard for people to change?

....

....

2. The Bible tells us that Christ came to change peoples' lives. What changes do these verses say take place because of Christ's love in our lives?

Romans 8:1,2 ....

Romans 8:15 ....

Romans 12:1,2 ....

2 Corinthians 5:17 ....

Ephesians 4:23,24 ....

Colossians 1:21,22 ....

3. First John 4:7,8 describes in three stages how change takes place in our lives. Fill in the blanks.
Stage One:
"Dear Friends, let us love one another for

....

When did you first begin to feel God's love in your life?

....

....

Stage Two:
"Everyone who loves

....

What is a sign that someone has become a Christian?

....

....

**TRANSFORMATION:
CHRIST CAME TO
CHANGE LIVES
COMPLETELY**

Stage Three:
...has been born of God ....

What is the result of being loved by God?

....

....

4. **Take a look at the people in your group. Identify one way you have seen each other changed because of God's love.**

....

....

SO WHAT?

Christ came to change our lives completely. He desires to leave no area untouched. Evaluate yourself in the areas of change listed below to see how much you've changed since Christ came into your life.

Take a couple of minutes alone right now to consider the following areas of your life. How has knowing Christ changed you? If you haven't really changed in that area *yet*, consider in what way you can begin to reflect God's life-changing love in your life.

Time: ....

Values: ....

Language: ....

Jokes: ....

Friends: ....

Enemies: ....

Music: ....

Opposite Sex: ....

Dating: ....

Parents: ....

School: ....

Church: ....

Attitudes: ....

Prayerfully consider one area in which you know you need to change and write down one step you will take in this area in the next week.

....

In your small group pray for one another concerning the area each of you has chosen to work on.

**TRANSFORMATION:
CHRIST CAME TO
CHANGE LIVES
COMPLETELY**

THINGS TO THINK ABOUT

1. What are the biggest changes you have made in your life this past year?

....

....

....

2. What are two areas of change you can work on this next year?

....

....

....

3. What are some specific action steps you can begin to practice today that will help those changes occur?

....

....

....

TRANSFORMATION: CHRIST CAME TO CHANGE LIVES COMPLETELY

PARENT PAGE

A FAMILY PHOTO OPPORTUNITY

Gather some of your oldest and newest favorite family photos.

1. Share one great memory from the photos in front of you.

....

....

2. Compare the old photos with the new ones. What are some of the most obvious changes that have taken place through the years?

....

....

3. One obvious change that takes place is actual physical growth. When people grow up, they often grow out of their old clothes. When they exchange those old clothes for new ones, they must take off the old clothes and put on the new. In Ephesians 4:22-24, Paul discusses those same two steps applied to a life change in Christ. What are those two steps?

   a. ....

   ....

   b. ....

   ....

4. Who does the verse say we are changing to be like?

....

....

5. In other words the new clothes have been laid out for us, all we must do is put them on. Share with each other three areas of your old life that have been the most difficult to put off.

....

....

6. If a photo could be taken of your spiritual life, what new changes would we see compared to a "photo" of your old life?

....

....

Session 2 "Transformation: Christ Came to Change Lives Completely"

Date ....

OUR NEW IDENTITY IN CHRIST

KEY VERSES

"For you did not receive a spirit that makes you a slave again to fear, but you received the Spirit of sonship. And by him we cry, 'Abba, Father.' The Spirit himself testifies with our spirit that we are God's children." Romans 8:15,16

BIBLICAL BASIS

Genesis 1:27,28; 2:25; 3:2,6-8, 10-13,22-24; 4:8,9;
Psalm 146:2,3; Proverbs 3:5,6;
John 3:16;
Romans 6:23;8:15,16,31-39;
1 Corinthians 1:2;
2 Corinthians 5:17,19,20;
Ephesians 1:3-10,13,14

THE BIG IDEA

When we become Christians, our identity is instantaneously changed from sinners to saints, from orphans to heirs.

AIMS OF THIS SESSION

During this session you will guide students to:
• Examine their identity outside of Christ;
• Discover their identity in Christ;
• Implement a new-you confidence.

WARM UP

YOUR FAMILY TREE—
Students fill in their family trees.

TEAM EFFORT— JUNIOR HIGH/ MIDDLE SCHOOL

AFFIRMALOPES—
Students write affirming words to one another.

TEAM EFFORT— HIGH SCHOOL

LET ME TELL YOU!—
Students make affirming statements about each other.

IN THE WORD

OUR SPIRITUAL HERITAGE—
A Bible study about our heritage through Christ.

THINGS TO THINK ABOUT (OPTIONAL)

Questions to get students thinking and talking about their insecurities in relationship to their inheritance in Christ.

PARENT PAGE

A tool to get the session into the home and allow parents and young people to discuss their own insecurities.

OUR NEW
IDENTITY IN CHRIST

LEADER'S DEVOTIONAL

"I will praise the Lord all my life; I will sing praise to my God as long as I live. Do not put your trust in princes, in mortal men, who cannot save" (Psalm 146:2,3).

I come from a large family. I'm one of two boys and five sisters in a wild family of seven siblings. Now that I have two little girls and a little boy on the way, our family-at-large is rapidly growing exponentially. My two daughters already have eighteen cousins and we're still counting....

Bringing new life into the world is what makes youth ministry so exciting. As teenagers receive new birth in Christ, you are in the enviable position of seeing their identity in Christ grow and develop. Watching and being able to experience the process of helping a young person grow as a Christian is a privilege and high calling. Those first few days, weeks and months are critical in a teenager's faith development as Satan will attempt to unravel God's work in his or her life. Just like a shepherd leading, protecting and guiding new lambs to safe pasture, shepherding teenagers plays a major role in their spiritual growth as God works in and through you to minister to their needs.

Just as important, if not more important, to young people developing their identity in Christ, is the continual growth of your identity in Christ. You need to be affirmed, encouraged, nurtured and inspired in your walk with Christ just as much as your young people do. Right now, who is investing time and energy in you and your relationship with God? Who are your mentors—the people who encourage you? Who are your role models? Who do you go to for spiritual counsel and guidance?

Youth workers need to be reminded about their identity in Christ too. Sit down with a friend to read over some of the verses in this lesson, and discuss how they have an impact on your life. (Do this apart from preparing for the lesson!) Your birth in Christ was a life-changing event that you don't want to forget. Nurturing your identity in Christ is the only way to keep growing closer to Him. (Written by Joey O'Connor.)

"The true center for self is Jesus Christ."
—Oswald Chambers

OUR NEW IDENTITY IN CHRIST

K EY VERSES

"For you did not receive a spirit that makes you a slave again to fear, but you received the Spirit of sonship. And by him we cry, 'Abba, Father.' The Spirit himself testifies with our spirit that we are God's children." Romans 8:15,16

B IBLICAL BASIS

Genesis 1:27,28; 2:25; 3:2,6-8,10-13,22-24; 4:8,9; Psalm 146:2,3; Proverbs 3:5,6; John 3:16; Romans 6:23; 8:15,16,31-39; 1 Corinthians 1:2; 2 Corinthians 5:17,19,20; Ephesians 1:3-10,13,14

T HE BIG IDEA

When we become Christians, our identity is instantaneously changed from sinners to saints, from orphans to heirs.

W ARM UP (5-10 MINUTES)

YOUR FAMILY TREE
• Give each student a copy of "Your Family Tree" on page 39 and a pen or pencil.
• Have students fill in their family trees.
Fill in the blanks on your family tree with the names of your relatives.

T EAM EFFORT—JUNIOR HIGH/
MIDDLE SCHOOL (15-20 MINUTES)

AFFIRMALOPES
• Arrange students in circles with about six students in each circle.
• Give each student an envelope with several slips of paper in it and a pen or pencil.
• Give the following directions:
"You will be writing down positive statements to describe your fellow group members. Remember this guideline: The statements must be affirming, positive, encouraging and in one sentence.
"Write your name on the front of the envelope. When I say go, pass your envelope to the person on your right and take the envelope from the person on your left. Write on a slip of

— Fold —

---

1. A brand new creation—2 Corinthians 5:17

1	2	3	4	5	6	7	8	9	10

I see myself through my lenses.   I see myself through God's lenses.

2. Sealed by the Holy Spirit as a loved child of God—Ephesians 1:13,14

1	2	3	4	5	6	7	8	9	10

I see myself through my lenses.   I see myself through God's lenses.

3. A sanctified saint—1 Corinthians 1:2

1	2	3	4	5	6	7	8	9	10

I see myself through my lenses.   I see myself through God's lenses.

4. Completely forgiven, holy and blameless—Ephesians 1:4

1	2	3	4	5	6	7	8	9	10

I see myself through my lenses.   I see myself through God's lenses.

5. Christ's ambassador—2 Corinthians 5:19,20

1	2	3	4	5	6	7	8	9	10

I see myself through my lenses.   I see myself through God's lenses.

SO WHAT?

What three specific areas of insecurity influence the way you act? Complete the following sentences:

1. I feel _____, so I _____
2. I feel _____, so I _____
3. I feel _____, so I _____

Referring to those same three insecurities, fill in the following sentences; this time apply the truth that we have learned about God's perspective. Feel free to ask for some help from your leader(s), others in your small group or God.

1. I feel _____, but God sees me as _____ so I am _____
2. I feel _____, but God sees me as _____ so I am _____
3. I feel _____, but God sees me as _____ so I am _____

T HINGS TO THINK ABOUT (OPTIONAL)
• Use the questions on page 43 after or as part of "In the Word."
1. What do you think your friends might be basing their identities on?

2. How do you think God feels about you now that you are in Christ?

3. How do you need to view other Christians who, like you, have a new identity in Christ?

P ARENT PAGE
• Distribute page to parents.

(1) **IN THE WORD**
OUR SPIRITUAL HERITAGE (25-30 MINUTES)

- Divide students into groups of three or four.
- Give each student a copy of "In the Word" on pages 40-42 and a pen or pencil, or display a copy using an overhead projector.
- Have students complete the Bible study.

(2) **TEAM EFFORT—HIGH SCHOOL** (15-20 MINUTES)

LET ME TELL YOU!

- Give each student a 3x5-inch index card and a pen or pencil.
- Give the following directions:

In this exercise you are going to affirm each group member by telling each other who you think they are.

1. Write the following on your card placing your name in the blank space:

"Hi, my name is _____. Who do you think I am?"

2. When you have finished writing on your card, I will collect them.
3. I will give the cards out again, but make sure you do not get your own card back.
4. The person wearing the most red will begin by reading the card in his or her hand and answering the question for the person whose name is on the card. The answers must be about who the person is, not about what they do. For example: Judy, you are compassionate. Jack, you are sensitive.
5. We will continue the exercise by having the person whose card was just read, read the card in his or her hand and so on until all the people in the group have had their question answered.
- If there is time, go ahead and pass out the cards again.
- Discuss the following questions:
1. What is one thing you know about yourself that defines who you are?
2. Some people say we grow up to be like the most influential people in our lives. Do you agree with that? Explain your answer.
3. Who is a person that you respect? Name one important quality that you respect in that person and why that quality is important to you.

paper an answer to this question: "Who do you think I am?" about the person whose name is on the envelope. The answer needs to be about who the person is, not what the person does. For example: Judy is a loving friend. Paul is a great listener. Don't sign the slips. It needs to be anonymous. You will have about 30 seconds for each statement. I will tell you when to pass each envelope. Go."

- Every 30 seconds tell the students to pass the envelopes.
- When each student has his or her envelope back, tell them: "Go ahead and look at what people wrote about who they think you are."
- Discuss the following questions:
1. What is something someone wrote about you that you have never thought about before?
2. How does it feel to be affirmed?

---- Fold ----

WHO WE WERE IN THE BEGINNING!

1. Read the verses. Draw a line from each verse to its matching statement.

Guilt-filled	Genesis 1:28
Shame-filled and afraid of God	Genesis 3:13
Without shame and free	Genesis 1:27
Rulers over all creatures	Genesis 2:25
Blame throwers	Genesis 4:8,9
Made by God in His own image	Genesis 3:23,24
Able to be deceived	Genesis 3:7,8
Knowing good and evil	Genesis 3:11-13
Banished from paradise	Genesis 3:10
Capable of sin and evil	Genesis 3:22
Lying to God	

2. How do you feel knowing that Adam and Eve were the first people on the earth from whom all people are descended—were once in paradise free from pain and sin and in intimate relationship with God the Father and Creator but because of a wrong choice they made, we are now all capable of shame, sin and rejection of God?

3. When the enemy deceived Adam and Eve into disobeying God, what do you think was the enemy's goal?

WHO WE BECAME AFTER THE FIRST SIN!

4. Adam and Eve were the first people on the earth who sinned by disobeying God's will. All people are born with the same sin nature—that is, they are spiritually dead, incapable of pleasing God and have a disposition to sin. In Romans 6:23, what does Paul say is the result of having a disposition to sin?

5. Spiritual death is separation from God's love. According to Romans 6:23 and John 3:16, what did God do to defeat spiritual death and to restore our relationship with Him?

WHO YOU ARE!

1. Read the passage below circling the following statements: "in Christ," "in Him," "through Him" and "in love" every time you read them.

2. From this passage, list what we receive under these categories:

In Christ?   In Him?   Through Him?   In love?

GOD'S LENSES OR MY LENSES

In Christ we go from broken sinners to completed saints. We go from loveless orphans to beloved children of God the Father. We go from old lives to brand new lives. These transformations come because of belief in Christ, the Son of God. It sometimes takes us awhile to see ourselves the way that God sees us. On a scale from 1 to 10, being "I see myself through my lenses," and 10 being "I see myself through God's lenses," rate yourself on the following "I See" scale. Have different members in your group look up and read out loud each verse for a better understanding of each new identity title, then take a moment to privately rate yourself.

OUR NEW
IDENTITY IN CHRIST

WARM UP

YOUR FAMILY TREE

Fill in the blanks on your family tree with the names of your relatives.

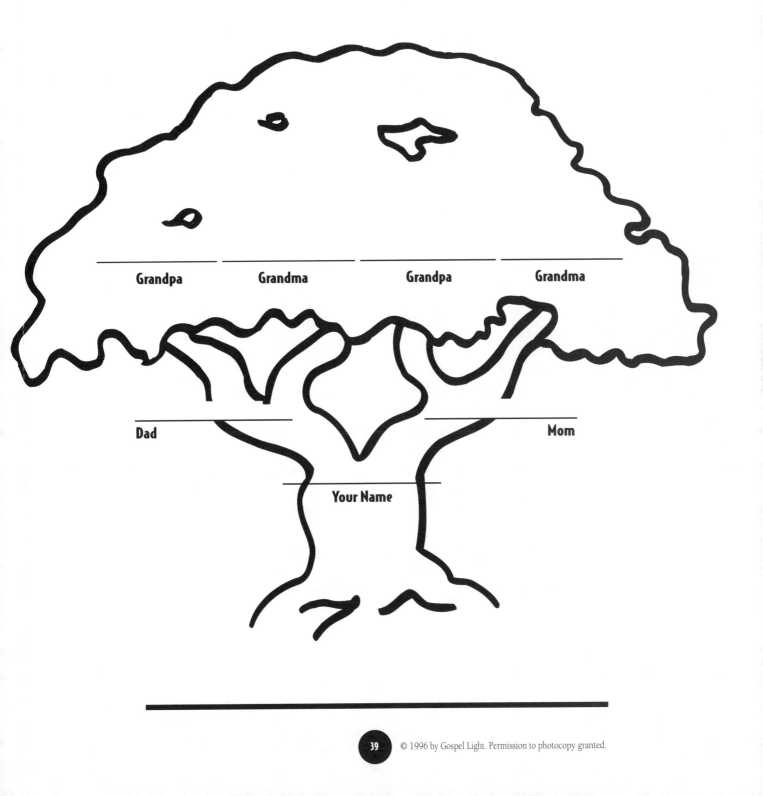

Grandpa   Grandma   Grandpa   Grandma

Dad   Mom

Your Name

**OUR NEW
IDENTITY IN CHRIST**

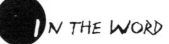

 N THE WORD

OUR SPIRITUAL HERITAGE

1. Read the verses. Draw a line from each verse to its matching statement.

Who We Were in the Beginning!

Without shame and free	Genesis 1:28
Rulers over all creatures	Genesis 1:27
Made by God in His own image	Genesis 2:25

Who We Became After the First Sin!

Guilt-filled	Genesis 3:6
Shame-filled and afraid of God	Genesis 3:13
Blame throwers	Genesis 4:8,9
Able to be deceived	Genesis 3:23,24
Knowing good and evil	Genesis 3:7,8
Banished from paradise	Genesis 3:11-13
Capable of sin and evil	Genesis 3:10
Lying to God	Genesis 3:22

2. How do you feel knowing that Adam and Eve—from whom all people are descended—were once in paradise free from pain and sin and in intimate relationship with God the Father and Creator, but because of a wrong choice they made we are now all capable of shame, sin and rejection of God?

....

....

3. When the enemy deceived Adam and Eve into disobeying God, what do you think was the enemy's goal?

....

....

4. Adam and Eve were the first people on the earth who sinned by disobeying God's will. All people born after them are born with the same sin nature—that is, they are spiritually dead, incapable of pleasing God and have a disposition to sin. In Romans 6:23, what does Paul say is the result of having a disposition to sin?

....

....

5. Spiritual death is separation from God's love. According to Romans 6:23 and John 3:16, what did God do to defeat spiritual death and to restore our relationship with Him?

....

....

....

Who You Are!

1. Read the passage below circling the following statements: "in Christ," "in Him," "through Him" and "in love" every time you read them.

> "Praise be to the God and Father of our Lord Jesus Christ, who has blessed us in the heavenly realms with every spiritual blessing in Christ. For he chose us in him before the creation of the world to be holy and blameless in his sight. In love he predestined us to be adopted as his sons through Jesus Christ, in accordance with his pleasure and will—to the praise of his glorious grace, which he has freely given us in the One he loves. In him we have redemption through his blood, the forgiveness of sins, in accordance with the riches of God's grace that he lavished on us with all wisdom and understanding. And he made known to us the mystery of his will according to his good pleasure, which he purposed in Christ, to be put into effect when the times will have reached their fulfillment— to bring all things in heaven and on earth together under one head, even Christ" (Ephesians 1:3-10).

2. From this passage, list what we receive under these categories:

In Christ?	In Him?	Through Him?	In Love?
....	....	....	....
....	....	....	....

God's Lenses or My Lenses

In Christ we go from broken sinners to completed saints. We go from loveless orphans to beloved children of God the Father. We go from old lives to brand new lives. These transformations come because of belief in Christ, the Son of God.

It sometimes takes us awhile to see ourselves the way that God sees us. On a scale from 1 to 10, 1 being "I see myself through my lenses" and 10 being "I see myself through God's lenses," rate yourself on the following "I See" scale. Have different members in your group look up and read out loud each verse for a better understanding of each new identity title, then take a moment to privately rate yourself.

1. A brand new creation—2 Corinthians 5:17

1	2	3	4	5	6	7	8	9	10

I see myself through my lenses.   I see myself through God's lenses.

2. Sealed by the Holy Spirit as a loved child of God—Ephesians 1:13,14

1	2	3	4	5	6	7	8	9	10

I see myself through my lenses.   I see myself through God's lenses.

3. A sanctified saint—1 Corinthians 1:2

1	2	3	4	5	6	7	8	9	10

I see myself through my lenses.   I see myself through God's lenses.

4. Completely forgiven, holy and blameless—Ephesians 1:4

1	2	3	4	5	6	7	8	9	10

I see myself through my lenses.   I see myself through God's lenses.

OUR NEW IDENTITY IN CHRIST

5. Christ's ambassador—2 Corinthians 5:19,20

1	2	3	4	5	6	7	8	9	10

I see myself through my lenses.   I see myself through God's lenses.

So What?

Your actions and attitudes demonstrate how you view yourself. Proverbs 3:5,6 tells us we can trust in our ways or we can trust God's ways. When we trust in God's ways, we see ourselves for who we, in truth, are.

Our victory comes in the practice of applying God's truth to our insecurities.

Identifying the Lie

What three specific areas of insecurity influence the way you act? Complete the following sentences:

> Example: I feel like a failure, so I'm afraid to try new things.
>
> I feel unlovable, so I act like I don't need people.

1. I feel .... , so I ....
2. I feel .... , so I ....
3. I feel .... , so I ....

Applying the Truth

Referring to those same three insecurities, fill in the following sentences; this time apply the truth that we have learned about God's perspective. Feel free to ask for some help from your leader(s), others in your small group or God.

> Example: I feel like a failure, but God sees me as a winner, so I am a winner.
>
> I feel unlovable, but God sees me as lovable so I am lovable.

1. I feel .... , but God sees me as ....

   so I am ....

2. I feel .... , but God sees me as ....

   so I am ....

3. I feel .... , but God sees me as ....

   so I am ....

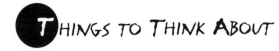 **T**HINGS TO THINK ABOUT

1. What do you think your friends might be basing their identities on?

....

....

....

2. How do you think God feels about you now that you are in Christ?

....

....

....

3. How do you need to view other Christians who, like you, have a new identity in Christ?

....

....

....

OUR NEW IDENTITY IN CHRIST

PARENT PAGE

OUR FAMILY PICTURE

Draw a picture of your family in the space below. Make the drawings fairly large and leave space between the figures. Under each family member's picture have that member write a word that best describes an insecure feeling that he or she has toward him- or herself.

1. According to Romans 8:31-37, who is on our side in the battle against our insecurities and what are the implications to help you deal with those insecurities?

   ....

   ....

2. Share why you think it is hard to get rid of your insecurities.

   ....

   ....

3. What does verse 37 say we are in light of our insecurities?

   ....

   ....

4. According to Romans 8:37-39, where should a believer's security be placed?

   ....

   ....

Reread Romans 8:31-39 together. Help each other conquer these insecurities by scribbling over each word in the drawing and replacing it with the truth that you see in God's all-conquering love.

Session 3 "Our New Identity in Christ"
Date ....

PLUGGING IN TO GOD'S POWER

KEY VERSES

"I pray that out of his glorious riches he may strengthen you with power through his Spirit in your inner being, so that Christ may dwell in your hearts through faith."
Ephesians 3:16,17

BIBLICAL BASIS

Joshua 1:9;
Psalm 150:1,2;
Ecclesiastes 4:9-12;
Matthew 17:20;
Luke 22:39-46;
John 14:12;
1 Corinthians 15:33;
Ephesians 3:14-20; 6:10,11;
Philippians 4:13;
2 Timothy 3:16,17;
Hebrews 10:22-25;
James 1:5-7;
1 John 4:3,4

THE BIG IDEA

We are guaranteed the power to overcome any opposition we might face in our life through maintaining our power connections to Christ.

AIMS OF THIS SESSION

During this session you will guide students to:
• Examine God's personal power;
• Discover three power connections that bring God's power into our lives;
• Implement a power connection plan.

WARM UP

CHECKING THE POWER METER—
Students discover how much power God can supply to believers.

TEAM EFFORT— JUNIOR HIGH/ MIDDLE SCHOOL

POWER PULL—
A game to find out which group is the most powerful—guys or girls.

TEAM EFFORT— HIGH SCHOOL

POUNDING POWER RELAY—
A game to illustrate power.

IN THE WORD

MAKING THE CONNECTION—
A Bible study on God's power and how to plug in to it.

THINGS TO THINK ABOUT (OPTIONAL)
Questions to get students thinking and talking about how they can improve their connections with God.

PARENT PAGE

A tool to get the session into the home and allow parents and young people to discuss what Jesus did when He was experiencing a "power outage."

PLUGGING IN TO GOD'S POWER

LEADER'S DEVOTIONAL

"Praise God in his sanctuary; praise him in his mighty heavens. Praise him for his acts of power; praise him for his surpassing greatness" (Psalm 150:1,2).

When I was in junior high, I had the unfortunate and painful experience of discovering the power of electricity the hard way. One evening I walked into the garage to get some clothes out of the dryer. On the cement floor next to the dryer was a small puddle of water. Remember this: water + a short circuit in a running dryer + barefeet = Yeeooww! The instant I stepped in the water and opened the dryer door, electricity came zapping up my arm like a bolt of white-hot lightning. It wasn't until my hair was standing up that my mind registered a panicked red alert. I jumped back from the dryer, screaming all sorts of high voltage words.

Getting zapped by our old dryer was the equivalent of the Energizer Bunny compared to electricity's true power. It's the difference between two "D" batteries and a power station for a major U.S. city. In the same way, the difference between God's power and Satan's power...well, there is no comparison.

Studying the power of God, wait...scratch that, experiencing the power of God is an awesome event in the life of a Christian. That's what makes this lesson on God's unlimited power so exciting. Knowing the power of God and how to get in touch with God through prayer, studying Scripture and spending time with other Christians is what makes the truth of this lesson so important. Power brings confidence. Once your students understand and experience the power of God in their lives, they won't fear the limited power of Satan.

One of the best ways for teenagers to grasp the power of God is to first see and hear about it in others' lives. I've often thought that students learned more from hearing what God has done in one another's lives than in listening to another of my Bible studies. Hearing one of their peers share how God has given them the strength to stop drinking or to get along with their parents is a living demonstration of God's power at work. For young people to be convinced of God's power, they must see concrete changes in other peoples' lives and their own. We must remember that we are living testimonials of God's power. We are no different than the people God used in the Old and New Testaments to accomplish His perfect work. God worked in powerful ways then; He still works in amazing ways today.

Why not take some time to reflect on God's power in your life? How has He demonstrated His power in your life lately? What kinds of changes has His power made in your life? Letting young people see God's power at work in your life is a solid way to get His current running in their lives. (Written by Joey O'Connor.)

"The Scriptures teach us the best way of living, the noblest way of suffering, and the most comfortable way of dying."
—John Flavel

PLUGGING IN TO GOD'S POWER

K EY VERSES

"I pray that out of his glorious riches he may strengthen you with power through his Spirit in your inner being, so that Christ may dwell in your hearts through faith." Ephesians 3:16,17

B IBLICAL BASIS

Joshua 1:9; Psalm 150:1,2; Ecclesiastes 4:9-12; Matthew 17:20; Luke 22:39-46; John 14:12; 1 Corinthians 15:33; Ephesians 3:14-20; 6:10,11; Philippians 4:13; 2 Timothy 3:16,17; Hebrews 10:22-25; James 1:5-7; 1 John 4:3,4

T HE BIG IDEA

We are guaranteed the power to overcome any opposition we might face in our life through maintaining our power connections to Christ.

W ARM UP (5-10 MINUTES)

CHECKING THE POWER METER

- Divide students into groups of four.
- Give each group a copy of "Checking the Power Meter" on page 49 and a pen or pencil.
- Have them complete the page.

Just how much power do Christians have? Look up each passage and write in the Power Meter what we have the power to do. The first one is done for you.

THE POWER METER

The Amps
Ephesians 3:20

John 14:12

Ephesians 6:10,11

Philippians 4:13

1 John 4:3,4

The Impact—As Believers We Have the Power to: do immeasurably more than we ask or imagine

Tear along perforation. Fold and place this Bible *Tuck-In*™ in your Bible for session use.

---

3. What does verse 7 say about a person who doubts God will answer?

The person who doubts is a person who approaches the Power Source trusting more in their own feelings—since doubt *is* a feeling—then in God. We need to approach our Power Source choosing to believe, regardless of how we feel, knowing God is faithful to those who believe.

Power Point Trust Test
When you go to the Power Source in prayer, what is your level of trust? Rate yourself on the following scale:

1	2	3	4	5
Doubt God Can				Believe God Can

II. Plug in to Power Partners

A. There are two types of power partners that believers can team up with. One is an "energizer," the other is an "energy eater."
According to Hebrews 10:24,25, what does an "energizer" do for a believer?

According to 1 Corinthians 15:33, what does an "energy eater" do for a believer?

B. You need two energizers—we recommend one your own age and a second at least four years older than you—to stay properly connected to the Power Source. What does Ecclesiastes 4:9-12 say about the need for a power partner?

II. Plug in to a Pack of Power People

A. Read Hebrews 10:25. What is the reason believers need a pack of power people?

B. It is difficult to stay strong out there in the world. A pack of power people can be a safe place to get recharged for the battle. What are some characteristics that help make your youth group a safe place where you like to go to be recharged?

C. What are some ways you can make your group a safe place to recharge your spiritual batteries?

T HINGS TO THINK ABOUT (OPTIONAL)

- Use the questions on page 53 after or as part of "In the Word."
1. What are five ways a believer can grow stronger in his or her relationship with Christ?

2. Has at least one of these ways made a big difference in your relationship with God? In what way? Share it with your group.

3. From the list you made choose one way to grow stronger in your relationship with Christ and write down what you will do this week. Be an energizer—pray for one another right now and through the coming week.

P ARENT PAGE

- Distribute page to parents.

TEAM EFFORT—JUNIOR HIGH/MIDDLE SCHOOL (15-20 MINUTES)

POWER PULL

- The object of the exercise is to see who is more powerful, the guys or the girls.
- The guys gather in a group on the floor in the middle of the room and grip onto each other as powerfully as possible.
- When the leader says go, the girls work together to separate the boys from each other's powerful grip. The girls must completely pull them from the group. Guidelines: Girls may not pull hair, tickle, gouge with long fingernails or pinch. Guys may not hit, slap or lose their cool. Remember: It is a game!
- The game continues until all the guys are separated or time is called.
- Discuss the following questions:

1. What made this game difficult?
2. Who were the hardest guys to pull apart? Why?
3. "Do not be terrified; do not be discouraged, for the Lord your God will be with you wherever you go" (Joshua 1:9). According to this verse, if God was on the guys' team, would the girls or anybody else be powerful enough to pull them apart? Explain your answer.

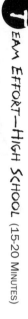

TEAM EFFORT—HIGH SCHOOL (15-20 MINUTES)

POUNDING POWER RELAY

- The object of the game is to be the first team to have its members move the grapefruit around the chair and back.
- Beforehand collect a pair of clean pantyhose and two grapefruits or softballs for as many teams as you think you will have.
- Divide students into even teams of about four to five members on each team.
- Have them line up one behind the other.
- Each team is given a pair of pantyhose with one grapefruit in one leg and one grapefruit is on the floor at the front of their line.
- Give the following directions:

1. When the leader says go, the first player slips the pantyhose onto his or her head and begins to pound the grapefruit on the floor moving it toward the chair. This is done by swinging the grapefruit-filled pantyhose from side to side or front to back while pounding the two grapefruits together.
2. The player pounds the grapefruit once around the chair and back to the line, passing the pantyhose to the next player and the process is repeated until the whole team is finished.
3. The first team to have all their players complete the relay wins.

- When the teams are finished, discuss the following questions:
1. What moved the grapefruit across the floor?
2. What made the grapefruit-filled pantyhose swing?
3. What was the goal of the game?

---

4. Jesus says to believers in Matthew 17:20 "If you have faith as small as a mustard seed, you can say to this mountain, 'Move from here to there,' and it will move. Nothing will be impossible for you." Who are we to have a mustard-seed-sized faith in?
5. What does Jesus say will be impossible for us when we have mustard-seed-sized, or even grapefruit-sized, faith in Him?
6. Ultimately, where does the power to move that mountain come from?

IN THE WORD (25-30 MINUTES)

MAKING THE CONNECTION

- Divide students into groups of three or four.
- Give each student a copy of "In the Word" on pages 50-53 and a pen or pencil, or display a copy using an overhead projector.
- Have students complete the Bible study.

PLUG IN TO THE POWER SOURCE

1. Hebrews 10:22 tells us to "draw near" to God. When we do draw near to God what is His response to us?
2. In Ephesians 3:14-19, Paul prays a prayer for believers. Read through the verses and circle the words that describe what believers can receive from our faithful God when we plug into Him as our Power Source.
3. Through whom and from where do we receive God's power?

4. Why does He give us His power?

THE POWER CONNECTIONS

With unlimited power at our disposal, believers need to:
1. Plug in to their Power Sources
   A. The Power Book—The Bible
   1. What does 2 Timothy 3:16 tell us about the source of all Scripture—the Power Book?

   2. What does Paul tell Timothy that Scripture is useful for?

   3. In verse 17, Paul calls a believer who plugs in through the Power Book a man of God. What will plugging in through the Power Book do for the believer?

   B. The Power Point—Prayer
   1. In James 1:5, James shares with believers about how to plug in to the Power Source through the power point called prayer. What does the verse say about prayer?

   2. There are two things to remember when we choose someone to ask for help. We must first believe in someone enough to risk asking for help. Second, we need to know that person well enough to expect the correct answer. What does verse 6 say is the reason we do not always receive what we ask of God?

 ARM UP

CHECKING THE POWER METER

Just how much power do Christians have? Look up each passage and write in the Power Meter what we have the power to do. The first one is done for you.

The Power Meter

The Amps	The Impact—As Believers We Have the Power to:
Ephesians 3:20	do immeasurably more than we ask or imagine

John 14:12

....

....

....

Ephesians 6:10,11

....

....

....

Philippians 4:13

....

....

....

1 John 4:3,4

....

....

....

IN THE WORD

MAKING THE CONNECTION

Plug in to the Power Source

1. Hebrews 10:22 tells us to "draw near" to God. When we do draw near to God what is His response to us?

....

....

2. In Ephesians 3:14-19, Paul prays a prayer for believers. Read through the verses and circle the words that describe what believers can receive from our faithful God when we plug into Him as our Power Source.

> "For this reason I kneel before the Father, from whom his whole family in heaven and on earth derives its name. I pray that out of his glorious riches he may strengthen you with power through his Spirit in your inner being, so that Christ may dwell in your hearts through faith. And I pray that you, being rooted and established in love, may have power, together with all the saints, to grasp how wide and long and high and deep is the love of Christ, and to know this love that surpasses knowledge—that you may be filled to the measure of all the fullness of God" (Ephesians 3:14-19).

3. Through whom and from where do we receive God's power?

....

....

4. Why does He give us His power?

....

....

The Power Connections

With unlimited power at our disposal, believers need to:

I. Plug in to Their Power Sources

    A. The Power Book—The Bible

        1. What does 2 Timothy 3:16 tell us about the source of all Scripture—the Power Book?

....

....

        2. What does Paul tell Timothy that Scripture is useful for?

....

3. In verse 17, Paul calls a believer who plugs in through the Power Book a man of God. What will plugging in through the Power Book do for the believer?

....

....

B. The Power Point—Prayer

1. In James 1:5, James shares with believers about how to plug into the Power Source through the power point called prayer. What does the verse say about prayer?

....

....

2. There are two things to remember when we choose someone to ask for help. We must first believe in someone enough to risk asking for help. Second, we need to know that person well enough to expect the correct answer from them. What does verse 6 say is the reason we do not always receive what we ask of God?

....

....

3. What does verse 7 say about a person who doubts God will answer?

....

....

The person who doubts is a person who approaches the Power Source trusting more in their own feelings—since doubt is a feeling—then in God. We need to approach our Power Source choosing to believe, regardless of how we feel, knowing God is faithful to those who believe.

Power Point Trust Test

When you go to the Power Source in prayer, what is your level of trust? Rate yourself on the following scale:

1	2	3	4	5
Doubt God Can				Believe God Can

II. Plug in to Power Partners

A. There are two types of power partners that believers can team up with. One is an "energizer," the other is an "energy eater."

According to Hebrews 10:24,25, what does an "energizer" do for a believer?

....

....

According to 1 Corinthians 15:33, what does an "energy eater" do for a believer?

....

....

**PLUGGING IN TO
GOD'S POWER**

IN THE WORD

B. You need two energizers—we recommend one your own age and a second at least four years older than you—to stay properly connected to the Power Source. What does Ecclesiastes 4:9-12 say about the need for a power partner?

....

....

III. Plug in to a Pack of Power People

A. Read Hebrews 10:25. What is the reason believers need a pack of power people?

....

....

B. It is difficult to stay strong out there in the world. A pack of power people can be a safe place to get recharged for the battle. What are some characteristics that help make your youth group a safe place where you like to go to be recharged?

....

....

C. What are some ways you can make your group a safe place to recharge your spiritual batteries?

....

....

So What?

A Power Connection Contract

Commitment One: Plugging in to the Power Source

Knowing that my success in standing against the scheme of the enemy depends on plugging in to the Power Source consistently, I...
commit to forming a Weekly Power Connection Plan that will include:

• Consistent time plugging in to the Power Book—the Bible.
• Consistent time plugging in to the power point—prayer.

I will read the Bible.. times a week, at... A.M./P.M.

I will pray.. minutes daily at... A.M./P.M.

Signed:... Date:..

Commitment Two: Plugging in to Two Power Partners

Knowing that my success in standing against the schemes of the enemy depends on plugging in to two power partners, I.. commit to finding:

• An energizer my own age to be one of my power partners.
• An energizer at least four years older and wiser than me to be my second power partner.

My peer power partner is... . We will meet

together.. .

My older power partner is... . We will meet

together.. .

Signed:...Date:.................................

Commitment Three: Plugging in to a Pack of Power People

Knowing that my success in standing against the schemes of the enemy depends on

plugging in to a pack of power people, I ....

commit to making my group the safest place possible by:

(i.e. Volunteering to be the group greeter, leading worship, etc.)

• ....

• ....

• ....

I commit to talking with my youth leader within one week from today about my

commitments.

Signed: ....Date:...

THINGS TO THINK ABOUT

1. What are five ways a believer can grow stronger in his or her relationship with Christ?

   ....

   ....

2. Has at least one of these ways made a big difference in your relationship with God? In what way? Share it with your group.

   ....

   ....

   ....

3. From the list you made choose one way to grow stronger in your relationship with Christ and write down what you will do this week. Be an energizer—pray for one another right now and through the coming week.

   ....

   ....

   ....

PLUGGING IN TO GOD'S POWER

PARENT PAGE

THE POWER IS OUT!

Share with each other a story about a time...
- When the lights went out in the house.
- When you ran out of gas.
- When the batteries went dead in your flashlight.
- When you ran out of firewood for a fire.
- When the wind died down.
- When you lost any type of power.

1. If you could have had anything during your moments of power outage, what would it have been?

....

....

Read together Luke 22:39-46. This is a time in Jesus' life when He is on His last bit of energy. Read the passage together trading off every verse.

2. What was going on in Jesus' life that caused Him to go to the Mount of Olives?

....

....

3. According to verse 39, He was going there...
   A. For the first time.
   B. Because His disciples were going and He decided to follow.
   C. Because He made a habit of it.
   D. Because He heard someone was going to be arrested and He didn't want to miss it.

4. What did Jesus do while He was there?

....

....

7. If you struggle with asking for the Father's help, what will it take for you to make a habit of going to Him daily for strength?

....

....

....

....

....

5. Jesus was facing a difficult decision in His life—one that would affect our lives as well as His. He went to His Father for the power to go on. How did God respond to His Son (see v. 43)?

....

....

6. We can have the strength to continue in difficult times by making a habit of going to the Father for power just as Jesus did. What is one difficult circumstance you are facing in your family that you need to take to the Father right now? Do it now!

....

....

Session 4 "Plugging in to God's Power"
Date ....

GOD IS GREATER

LEADER'S PEP TALK

As an example of the power of influential messages, I recently told a group of students in a drug and crisis rehabilitation clinic the results of being called a radish. "The truth is," I said, "that if I were to tell you each time I saw you—say five times a day—that you are a radish, you would eventually believe it. You would eventually get up in the morning, go to the mirror and see what you think is a radish."

One teen immediately responded, "No way, it is impossible to think you're a vegetable."

I said, "Maybe so, but what if every time I saw you, I were to say you were worthless."

At this point a question from one of the girls in the group struck me. She asked, "What if it's the truth? What if you really are worthless?"

I turned to her and said, "See you proved my point. A person can easily feel worthless because of the many messages she receives. But people are not worthless, people have worth." From the look on her face, I could tell that the truth hit home. Early in her life her biological father abandoned the family, only later to come back in her early teens and sexually molest her. She has spent a large part of her life searching for a lost love.

"The thief comes only to steal and kill and destroy" (John 10:10).

Spend any time at all with a group of teens, and it is evident that an enemy is at work in the lives of adolescents spiritually battling for their attention and souls. I feel convinced that educating your students in a balanced fashion about the truth of Satan and his demons is essential to their well-being.

This section of the study will lead you on a journey to discover the enemy's desires, motivations and schemes.

Christ has "come that they may have life, and have it to the full"

(John 10:10).

In this section you will also find victory in the power of a God who cares, and along with that victory comes abundant life.

God's best to you as you learn under the protection of a *greater* God.

SPIRITUAL WARFARE:
WHAT'S IT ALL ABOUT?

EY VERSE

"For our struggle is not against flesh and blood, but against the rulers, against the authorities, against the powers of this dark world and against the spiritual forces of evil in the heavenly realms." Ephesians 6:12

BIBLICAL BASIS

2 Chronicles 20:2-17;
Psalm 139:7-12;
Luke 4:1-13,31-36;
John 8:31,32,42-44; 10:10;
Romans 8:31-39;
2 Corinthians 10:3-6;
Ephesians 1:21-23; 2:1,2; 6:12-22;
Colossians 1:21-23;
James 2:19;
1 Peter 5:8;
Revelation 12:10

THE BIG IDEA

We can best equip ourselves to stand our ground against the enemy when we understand the whos, whats and wheres of the spiritual battle.

AIMS OF THIS SESSION

During this session you will guide students to:
• Examine where the battle takes place;
• Discover what and who the battle is for;
• Implement some war-winning action steps.

WARM UP

WHAT DO YOU THINK YOU KNOW?—
A word game to discover how much students know about the spiritual battle.

TEAM EFFORT— JUNIOR HIGH/ MIDDLE SCHOOL

WINK, YOU'RE DEAD!—
A game to demonstrate the spiritual battle.

TEAM EFFORT— HIGH SCHOOL

AGREE OR DISAGREE?—
Students demonstrate their agreement concerning statements about the enemy.

IN THE WORD

INVESTIGATIVE REPORTING—
A Bible study on spiritual warfare.

THINGS TO THINK ABOUT (OPTIONAL)

Questions to get students thinking and talking about the motives and methods of the devil and how God overcomes the devil's work.

PARENT PAGE

A tool to get the session into the home and allow parents and young people to discuss how spiritual warfare is affecting our society.

SPIRITUAL WARFARE: WHAT'S IT ALL ABOUT?

LEADER'S DEVOTIONAL

"You believe that there is one God. Good! Even the demons believe that—and shudder" (James 2:19).

One of my pet peeves is being with a group of people who are talking about a great movie I haven't seen yet. When it comes to knowing the details of a movie, what happens in the plot, what twists and turns the story takes, I don't want to know a thing. I want to see and experience the movie for myself. I don't want to know what happens in the end. I don't want to know who dies, who wins, who loses or who makes off with the money and the gorgeous girl who's ready to steal the money from whoever made off with it. I want to make my own evaluation of whether or not it was a good movie. I want to be surprised.

However, when dealing with spiritual matters, I don't want to be surprised at all. In spiritual warfare, you and I can't afford to be surprised. Being surprised at the movies is fine, but on the battlefield for our souls a surprise attack is the last thing we want. Understanding what goes on in the spiritual realms is absolutely necessary to walk with Christ. Why? If we ignore the spiritual forces of darkness, we are essentially leaving out a significant portion of life that Jesus encountered here on earth. Jesus faced Satan for 40 days alone in the desert. He cast demons out of a possessed man and commanded them into a herd of pigs. A large part of His healing ministry was spent casting out demons. Even the demons recognized Him, called out His name and shuddered at His voice. At the Passover meal the night He was betrayed, Jesus saw the work of Satan seize the heart of Judas that ultimately led Jesus to the cross. To ignore the reality of evil spiritual forces is foolishness; Jesus faced spiritual battles on a daily basis. As Christians, should we expect anything less?

As you spend time on campus or at church with teenagers, be aware of Satan's strategies against you, your ministry team and the students themselves. This lesson will pull no punches. You and your students will receive good, solid information on what spiritual warfare is all about. You'll find dozens of wonderful promises from God's word to equip you to understand how to stand strong in Christ. Fortunately, your students will learn the end of this exciting story: In Christ, we win and Satan loses. That's wonderful news even for someone who likes to wait till the very end to see who wins. (Written by Joey O'Connor.)

"We begin to need His help with every little thing and at every moment, because without it we can do nothing. The world, the flesh, and the devil wage a fierce and continuous war on our souls. If we weren't capable of humbly depending on God for assistance, our souls would be dragged down. Although this total dependence may sometimes go against our human nature, God takes great pleasure in it."
—Brother Lawrence

Tear along perforation. Fold and place this Bible *Tuck-In*™ in your Bible for session use.

SPIRITUAL WARFARE: WHAT'S IT ALL ABOUT?

 KEY VERSES

"For our struggle is not against flesh and blood, but against the rulers, against the authorities, against the powers of this dark world and against the spiritual forces of evil in the heavenly realms." Ephesians 6:12

B IBLICAL BASIS

2 Chronicles 20:2-17; Psalm 139:7-12; Luke 4:1-13, 31-36; John 8:31,32,42-44; 10:10; Romans 8:31-39; 2 Corinthians 10:3-6; Ephesians 1:21-23; 2:1,2; 6:12-22; Colossians 1:21-23; James 2:19; 1 Peter 5:8; Revelation 12:10

T HE BIG IDEA

We can best equip ourselves to stand our ground against the enemy when we understand the whos, whats and wheres of the spiritual battle.

W ARM UP (5-10 MINUTES)

What Do You Think You Know?

• Write the following puzzle on a chalkboard, whiteboard, poster or overhead transparency:
What do you think you know about the enemy?

d
e n e m y
c
e
i
v
e

• Ask for students to raise their hands if they know a word to describe the devil. Give them a piece of chalk or felt-tip pen and have them add their words to the puzzle one at a time connecting each word to the other words by at least one letter.
• As words are added, more words can be added on to the new words as well.
• Tell students "The more we know about the enemy, the better we will be at avoiding his influences in our lives."

— Fold —

John 10:10 ....

Romans 8:31-39 ....

Ephesians 2:1,2 ....

Colossians 1:21-23 ....

When your group has completed its research, write a paragraph or two as your part of the article on spiritual warfare.

Group Four
There are two armies involved in this spiritual battle. Who is the commander-in-chief of each army and what is each commander's primary weapon?

2 Chronicles 20:2-17 ....

Luke 4:1-13,31-36 ....

John 8:31,32,42-44 ....

John 10:10 ....

Romans 8:31-39 ....

2 Corinthians 10:3-6 ....

1 Peter 5:8 ....
When your group has completed its research, write a paragraph or two as your part of the article on spiritual warfare.

So WHAT?

1. What are some evidences you have seen that confirm that the war between God and the enemy is going on around us and within us daily?

2. In what ways have you personally experienced spiritual warfare?

3. What are two war-winning ways that you can practice this week to secure your protection from the evil one?

T HINGS TO THINK ABOUT (OPTIONAL)

• Use the questions on page 64 after or as part of "In the Word."

1. How can we know for sure there is a devil?

2. What are some ways that the devil wages war against Christians?

3. What are three ways God wages war against the devil?

P ARENT PAGE

• Distribute page to parents.

TEAM EFFORT—JUNIOR HIGH/ MIDDLE SCHOOL

WINK, YOU'RE DEAD! (15-20 MINUTES)

The object of the game is to identify the wink murderer before he or she murders you.

• You will need wooden matches—one for each student present—and a small cup or box.

• Pre-burn only one of the matches and put it in a small box or cup with the rest of the unburned matches. There needs to be enough matches so each student in the group gets one.

• Optional: Prepare small slips of paper folded in half with an M written inside one of the folded papers.

• Have the students sit in a circle facing each other.

• Pass the box or cup above the students' heads not allowing them to look into the box as they grab a match or slip of paper. No one should see the match or paper except the student who selected it.

• The person with the burnt match or M is the wink murderer.

• When the leader says go, the wink murderer looks around the circle at the other players trying to make eye contact. As the murderer makes eye contact with a player, they are to "murder" the player they are looking at by winking at them. The murderer's goal is to wink without being seen by anyone else except the murder victim. The victim can die as theatrical a death or as quiet a death as he or she likes. The victim just can't die in a way that will give away the identity of the murderer.

• The rest of the players are to be watching to see if they can guess the identity of the murderer without getting killed themselves.

• Repeat as much as time allows.

• Discuss the following questions:

1. The spiritual battles we fight and this game are a lot alike. In the game, what made it hard to stay alive?

2. What was the goal of the wink murderer?

• Tell the students "In the spiritual battle the goals are the same. The believer's goal is to identify the enemy and his tricks without getting his or her relationship with Christ killed. The enemy's goal is to inconspicuously lure you, a believer, away from life with Christ and to kill your faith in God."

TEAM EFFORT—HIGH SCHOOL (15-20 MINUTES)

AGREE OR DISAGREE?

• Using two sheets of 12x18-inch construction paper write the word "agree" in large letters on one sheet and the word "disagree" on the other one. Tape one sheet to the wall on one side of the room and the other to the wall on the opposite side.

• Tell students that you will read five statements to them and they are to decide whether or not they agree or disagree with each statement. When they decide, they are to walk to the side of the room labeled with the word describing that decision.

• After students make their choice, ask two or three of them on each side of the room to

explain why they made the choice they did alternating between those who agree and those who disagree if possible.

1. The devil is only a make-believe character.

2. There is evidence that the enemy is alive and active in our world today.

3. The enemy only hates Christians who are on fire for God.

4. The best way to stay away from spiritual warfare is to not grow in your relationship with Christ.

5. The enemy desires to destroy your relationship with a loving God.

IN THE WORD (25-30 MINUTES)

INVESTIGATIVE REPORTING

• In this study divide the students into four groups to write a portion of a newspaper article for *Hark the Angel Herald*. Each group is to study the verses in its section, answer the questions and then write their portion of the article based on their research.

• Provide each group with a copy of "In the Word" on pages 61-63, several sheets of paper and pens or pencils.

• After about 15 minutes, have each group read its article to the other groups.

Group One
Life for a Christian is a spiritual battle fought against spiritual forces. Who are the forces and where are the battles taking place?

Psalm 139:7-12 ....

Luke 4:31-36 ....

Romans 8:31-39 ....

Ephesians 1:21-23 ....

Ephesians 6:12,13 ....

1 Peter 5:8 ....

Revelation 12:10 ....

When your group has completed its research, write a paragraph or two as your part of the article on spiritual warfare.

Group Two
The battles are being fought for the soul and attention of believers. What are the strategies the enemy uses to attack Christians?

Luke 4:1-13 ....

John 8:43,44 ....

John 10:10 ....

Ephesians 2:1,2 ....

When your group has completed its research, write a paragraph or two as your part of the article on spiritual warfare.

Group Three
The enemy's army can steal daily victories from believers. By doing this what does the enemy actually hope to gain?

Fold

 **IN THE WORD**

INVESTIGATIVE REPORTING

Hark the Angel Herald

INTEROFFICE MEMO

Reporter's Story Request

To: Staff writers

From: Editor

Topic: Spiritual Warfare: What's It All About?

There has been an unusual amount of unexplained occurrences taking place in the Christian world. The word on the street is that it is something called "spiritual warfare." We need an article written on this and you're the perfect team to write it. I've taken the liberty to provide you with some references from the Bible. Study those references because they are as good as interviews with the people who wrote them. Gather the information and write a portion of the article confirming the truths and answering the questions below.

Group One

Life for a Christian is a spiritual battle fought against spiritual forces. Who are the forces and where are the battles taking place?

Psalm 139:7-12 ....

....

Luke 4:31-36 ....

....

Romans 8:31-39 ....

....

Ephesians 1:21-23 ....

....

Ephesians 6:12,13 ....

....

1 Peter 5:8 ....

....

Revelation 12:10 ....

....

When your group has completed its research, write a paragraph or two as your part of the article on spiritual warfare.

IN THE WORD

Group Two
The battles are being fought for the soul and attention of believers. What are the strategies the enemy uses to attack Christians?

Luke 4:1-13 ....

....

John 8:43,44 ....

....

John 10:10 ....

....

Ephesians 2:1,2 ....

....

When your group has completed its research, write a paragraph or two as your part of the article on spiritual warfare.

Group Three
The enemy's army can steal daily victories from believers. By doing this what does the enemy actually hope to gain?

John 10:10 ....

....

Romans 8:31-39 ....

....

Ephesians 2:1-2 ....

....

Colossians 1:21-23 ....

....

When your group has completed its research, write a paragraph or two as your part of the article on spiritual warfare.

Group Four
There are two armies involved in this spiritual battle. Who is the commander-in-chief of each army and what is each commander's primary weapon?

2 Chronicles 20:2-17 ....

....

Luke 4:1-13,31-36 ....

....

N THE WORD

John 8:31,32,42-44 ....

....

John 10:10 ....

....

Romans 8:31-39 ....

....

2 Corinthians 10:3-6 ....

....

1 Peter 5:8 ....

....

When your group has completed its research, write a paragraph or two as your part of the article on spiritual warfare.

So What?

Christians in our nation have *not* been raised with the understanding that there is a spiritual realm in this world. They either dismiss the idea that spiritual warfare is real, or they choose to place it on a so-called spiritual level that is far beyond affecting us here on earth. In your small groups discuss the following questions:

1. What are some evidences you have seen that confirm that the war between God and the enemy is going on around and within us daily?

    ....

    ....

    ....

2. In what ways have you personally experienced spiritual warfare?

    ....

    ....

    ....

3. What are two war-winning ways that you can practice this week to secure your protection from the evil one?

    ....

    ....

    ....

THINGS TO THINK ABOUT

1. How can we know for sure there is a devil?

....
....
....

2. What are some ways that the devil wages war against Christians?

....
....
....

3. What are three ways God wages war against the devil?

....
....
....

PARENT PAGE

BATTLE STRATEGIES

We live in a world which is interested in spiritual things more than at any other time in history. What does 1 Peter 5:8 warn us about?

....

....

Parent: Adults often say, "Things are sure different now than when I was a kid." Share with your teen how you've seen the world become more evil and what the impact of this increase in evil has had on our society since your teen years.

CHECK THE TV LISTINGS

With your TV guide in hand, go through the week's listings and find 10 shows that are airing some type of spiritual dimension.

	Show	Spiritual Dimension
1.		
2.		
3.		
4.		
5.		
6.		
7.		
8.		
9.		
10.		

With a highlighter mark the shows that have a Christian dimension.

In 1 Peter 5:8, what are the two action steps that we can take to keep ourselves from getting caught up in the evil of our present world?

....

In light of your TV discoveries, what is one way believers can resist the enemy?

....

How does 1 Peter 5:8 tell believers to strengthen their faith?

....

What are two ways you can strengthen your personal faith this week?

....

Session 5 "Spiritual Warfare: What's It All About?" Date ....

THE PROFILE OF THE ENEMY

KEY VERSES

"For by him all things were created: things in heaven and on earth, visible and invisible, whether thrones or powers or rulers or authorities; all things were created by him and for him. He is before all things, and in him all things hold together."
Colossians 1:16,17

BIBLICAL BASIS

Genesis 1:1,31;
Isaiah 14:12-15;
Matthew 4:1-10;
John 1:3; 8:44; 10:10; 14:30;
Romans 8:38,39;
2 Corinthians 4:4; 11:14;
Ephesians 2:2;
Colossians 1:16,17;
1 Timothy 4:1;
Hebrews 12:4-6;
James 2:19;
1 Peter 5:8;
2 Peter 2:4;
1 John 4:4;
Revelation 12:7-10

THE BIG IDEA

The more information we have about the enemy, the easier it will be to beat him at his game.

AIMS OF THIS SESSION

During this session you will guide students to:
• Examine the origins of the enemy;
• Discover the enemy's personality traits;
• Implement a plan to avoid the enemy.

WARM UP

THE MYSTERY OF THE BROKEN WINDOW—
Students complete a story that illustrates how looks can be deceiving.

TEAM EFFORT— JUNIOR HIGH/ MIDDLE SCHOOL
WANTED: DEAD OR ALIVE—
Students develop posters to warn people about Satan.

TEAM EFFORT— HIGH SCHOOL
"SHUT DE DOOR"—
Discussion of a song describing Satan and his wiles.

IN THE WORD

EQUALLY STOKED: A COMPANY THAT BRINGS PERSONALITIES TOGETHER—
A Bible study on who Satan is and how he works.

THINGS TO THINK ABOUT (OPTIONAL)

Questions to get students thinking and talking about how to avoid Satan's influence.

PARENT PAGE

A tool to get the session into the home and allow parents and young people to discuss what they know about Satan.

THE PROFILE OF THE ENEMY

Leader's Devotional

"In your struggle against sin, you have not yet resisted to the point of shedding your blood. And you have forgotten that word of encouragement that addresses you as sons: 'My son, do not make light of the Lord's discipline, and do not lose heart when he rebukes you, because the Lord disciplines those he loves, and he punishes everyone he accepts as a son'" (Hebrews 12:4-6).

It doesn't take too long in youth ministry before you realize what you've probably suspected for some time: the battle becomes more intense. After working with teenagers, families, volunteer staff and other youth workers for over ten years, there is one verse I would pick to summarize Satan's mission on earth: John 10:10 warns us "'The thief comes only to steal and kill and destroy.'"

Some years ago, a fellow youth worker asked me, "Joey, if Satan were going to get you in one area, what would it be?" Ouch! Now that's a good question. I could probably name more areas than one. The main point of my friend's very pointed question is that we are all open to spiritual attack. We are all vulnerable to Satan's ploys. His desire is to steal, kill, and destroy our relationship with God.

Three strategies that I believe Satan uses to actively destroy youth workers are:

One: Discourage your spirit. Show me a tired, discouraged youth worker and I'll show you a plump, sitting duck for Satan's banquet table. Discouragement can close our heart to the voice of God as Satan tickles our ears with whispers of deceit. Discouragement raises its ugly head in such comments as, "What's the use? None of these kids care. No one would notice if I wasn't here. I'm not making any kind of difference in these kids lives."

Two: Discredit your ministry. It doesn't matter if you're a volunteer or paid youth minister, there will be problems, situations, conflicts and disagreements in your youth ministry that Satan will use in the attempt to discredit your ministry. People will challenge your motives, point out your weaknesses and draw battle lines against you. In an attempt to attack your character and integrity, Satan will fire criticism at you. The devil doesn't care whether it's true or not because he just wants to bring you down. Anything to pull your eyes off God and the work God has planned for you.

Three: Distance you from God. Along with discouragement, Satan will needle you with disappointment and disillusionment to distance you from God. Remember, Satan wants to kill, steal and destroy your friendship with Christ. Contrast that with Jesus' words in the second part of John 10:10, "'I have come that they may have life, and have it to the full.'"

If you are feeling any of these emotions or conflicts, remember that you're not fighting against flesh or blood. Grab a friend to pray with you and don't try to fight your battles alone. (Written by Joey O'Connor.)

**"Prayer is the mortar that holds our house together."
—St. Teresa**

THE PROFILE OF THE ENEMY

Key Verses

"For by him all things were created: things in heaven and on earth, visible and invisible, whether thrones or powers or rulers or authorities; all things were created by him and for him. He is before all things, and in him all things hold together." Colossians 1:16,17

Biblical Basis

Genesis 1:1,31; Isaiah 14:12-15; Matthew 4:1-10; John 1:3; 8:44; 10:10; 14:30; Romans 8:38,39; 2 Corinthians 4:4; 11:14; Ephesians 2:2; Colossians 1:16,17; 1 Timothy 4:1; Hebrews 12:4-6; James 2:19; 1 Peter 5:8; 2 Peter 2:4; 1 John 4:4; Revelation 12:7-10

The Big Idea

The more information we have about the enemy, the easier it will be to beat him at his game.

Warm Up (5-10 Minutes)

The Mystery of the Broken Window

- Have each student add one sentence to the end of the following story:
  At 3:41 P.M., I returned home from school after an exciting day of learning. As I walked toward the house, I noticed something unusual. There, in the large picture window at the front of our house was a huge hole. I ran to the front door, unlocked it and went in only to find broken glass and small pebbles surrounded by sand. The piece of evidence I was looking for was gone. I was almost positive someone had thrown a...
- After completing the story, discuss the following:
  Sometimes in familiar circumstances things occur that are difficult to explain. It is the enemy's talent to make things look different than they are. What is one circumstance that happens to people that could be a trick of the devil?

Fold

	Trait of the enemy	Evidence
Matthew 4:1	....	....
John 8:44	....	....
2 Corinthians 4:4	....	....
2 Corinthians 11:14	....	....
Ephesians 2:2	....	....
1 Timothy 4:1	....	....
James 2:19	....	....
1 Peter 5:8	....	....
Revelation 12:10	....	....

Complete the following sentence and write a paragraph using the information you have researched.

Examples of his activity

Matthew 4:1	....	....
John 8:44	....	....
2 Corinthians 4:4	....	....
2 Corinthians 11:14	....	....
Ephesians 2:2	....	....
1 Timothy 4:1	....	....
James 2:19	....	....
1 Peter 5:8	....	....
Revelation 12:10	....	....

Complete the following sentence and write a paragraph using the information you have researched.

Personal Ad Final Input Sheet

Client: Satan

Group Four: Satan's Activities and Hobbies

So What?

1. **What new information did you learn about the enemy?**

   ....

2. **What are two reasons why you wouldn't respond to the enemy's "Equally Stoked" ad?**

   ....

Things to Think About (Optional)

- Use the questions on page 77 after or as part of "In the Word."

1. **Where did the devil come from?**

   ....

2. **If you were to describe the enemy with several one-word descriptions, what words would you use and why?**

   ....

3. **What are some ways you can keep Satan from being your friend?**

   ....

Parent Page

- Distribute page to parents.

MIDDLE SCHOOL (15-20 MINUTES)

WANTED: DEAD OR ALIVE

- Divide students into groups of four or five.
- Give each group a few sheets of paper, a few felt-tip pens and a copy of "Wanted: Dead or Alive" on page 71, or display a copy using an overhead projector.

Your group is the law in these parts and you are on the look out for Satan. In order to nab the pesky critter you need to draw up a wanted poster, complete with a description of Satan, so folks will know how to spot him. On the poster make sure to answer these important questions.

1. What things were created by God?

2. Where have all things been created?

3. Specifically what did God create?

"SHUT DE DOOR"

- Play Randy Stonehill's song "Shut de Door" (on his Equator album) for the students and have them discuss the following questions:

1. What is the song about?

2. What does the song say Satan is?

3. What do you think it means to "shut the door"?

4. Why do we need to shut the door on Satan?

IN THE WORD (25-30 MINUTES)

EQUALLY STOKED: A COMPANY THAT BRINGS PERSONALITIES TOGETHER

- In this section your students will study the personality profile of the devil himself.
- Divide students into four groups.
- Give each group a copy of "In the Word" on pages 72-77 and pens or pencils.
- Each group will study one of the four sections in the personality profile, write a paragraph about their findings and read it to the rest of the group at the end of the study.

GROUP ONE: WHERE SATAN ORIGINATED

To begin, you will need to investigate two truths.

Truth One: All things were created by God.

Read Colossians 1:16,17 and answer the questions below.

1. What things were created by God?

2. Where have all things been created?

3. Specifically what did God create?

---

4. Read Genesis 1:1 and 31 and John 1:3. What information do these verses give you about where Satan originated?

Truth Two: God is in control of all things.

Read the following verses and answer these questions as you read them:

1. When the enemy goes head-to-head with God, who do these verses say will win?

2. Why does this truth make God a winner and the enemy a loser?

Romans 8:38,39

Colossians 1:17

1 John 4:4

GROUP TWO: SATAN'S BACKGROUND INFORMATION

Use the verses below as research material to find out as much as possible about Satan's background. Be sure to take notes on each verse so you can write the background section of the personal ad.

Isaiah 14:12-15

John 8:44

John 14:30

2 Corinthians 11:14

2 Peter 2:4

Revelation 12:7-9

Complete the following sentence and write a paragraph using the information you have researched.

GROUP THREE: SATAN'S PERSONALITY PROFILE

This is where you will find the real heart of the client's personality. Do your research, keeping track of those key traits that make a personality profile come alive.

Matthew 4:1-10

John 8:44

2 Corinthians 4:4

2 Corinthians 11:14

Ephesians 2:2

1 Timothy 4:1

James 2:19

1 Peter 5:8

Revelation 12:10

Complete the following sentence and write a paragraph using the information you have researched.

GROUP FOUR: SATAN'S ACTIVITIES AND HOBBIES

Who the enemy is dictates what the enemy does. Using the verses below identify 11 traits of the enemy. From these traits identify two specific examples of the enemy's activity in the world in which you live.

Fold

 **T**EAM EFFORT

WANTED: DEAD OR ALIVE

Your group is the law in these parts and you are on the look out for Satan. In order to nab the pesky critter you need to draw up a wanted poster, complete with a description of Satan, so folks will know how to spot him.

On the poster make sure to answer these important questions.

1. **Who is he?**

....

....

....

2. **What's he wanted for?**

....

....

....

3. **Why is he dangerous?**

....

....

....

4. **What are his weapons?**

....

....

....

5. **How will people know when they see him?**

....

....

....

THE
PROFILE OF THE
ENEMY

IN THE WORD

EQUALLY STOKED: A COMPANY THAT BRINGS PERSONALITIES TOGETHER

Group One: Where Satan Originated

You are on the staff of a nationally known companionship company called "Equally Stoked" that links personalities together based on their origins, personality traits, activities and hobbies. Your job is to gather information and write your portion of a personal ad to go in their national members resource book. Today you will research and write a section of the ad about where Satan originated. First research your group's information, then write that section of the ad on the "Personal Ad Final Input Sheet."

To begin, you will need to investigate two truths.

Truth One: All things were created by God.
Read Colossians 1:16,17 and answer the questions below.

1. What things were created by God?

....

....

....

2. Where have all things been created?

....

....

....

3. Specifically what did God create?

....

....

....

4. Read Genesis 1:1 and 31 and John 1:3. What information do these verses give you about where Satan originated?

....

....

....

Truth Two: God is in control of all things.
Read the following verses and answer the following questions:

1. When the enemy goes head-to-head with God, who do these verses say will win?

....

....

2. Why does this truth make God a winner and the enemy a loser?

Romans 8:38,39 ....

Colossians 1:17 ....

1 John 4:4 ....

Complete the following sentence and write a paragraph using the information you have researched.

Personal Ad Final Input Sheet

Client: Satan

Group One: Where Satan Originated

Hi!, I'm Satan and I'm originally from... ....

....

....

....

....

Group Two: Satan's Background Information

You are on the staff of a nationally known companionship company called "Equally Stoked" that links personalities together based on their origins, personality traits, activities and hobbies. Your job is to gather information and write your portion of a personal ad to go in their national members resource book. Today you will research and write a section of the ad about Satan's background. First research your group's information, then write that section of the ad on the "Personal Ad Final Input Sheet."

If Satan is one of God's creation, then how did he turn out to be evil and become an enemy of God? This is a question that many scholars have wrestled with for years. It is some theologians' interpretation that the devil was God's greatest angel, who was on a power trip wanting to be like God or greater than God and rule the universe. In his attempt at greatness, he led a revolt of angels in heaven and successfully tempted man in the garden scoring a heavy hit on God's love-filled plan. By going against God, he and his army of demons were disobedient and cast out of heaven to dwell in darkness. Let's look at some verses the theologians have studied to come up with that interpretation.

Use the following verses as research material to find out as much as possible about Satan's background. Be sure to take notes on each verse so you can write the background section of the personal ad.

THE
PROFILE OF THE
ENEMY

Isaiah 14:12-15 ....

John 8:44 ....

John 14:30 ....

2 Corinthians 11:14 ....

2 Peter 2:4 ....

Revelation 12:7-9 ....

A helpful side note: What we don't know for sure is exactly how the devil went from being created by God—assumed to be good—to becoming God's enemy. We don't have to know how the enemy came to be to know that the enemy is real and a threat to the life that Christ has planned for Christians.

Complete the following sentence and write a paragraph using the information you have researched.

Personal Ad Final Input Sheet

Client: Satan

Group Two: Satan's Background Information

Hi!, I'm Satan and I'd like to tell you a little about myself. I... ....

....

....

....

....

....

....

....

....

....

Group Three: Satan's Personality Profile

You are on the staff of a nationally-known companionship company called "Equally Stoked" that links personalities together based on their origins, personality traits, activities and hobbies. Your job is to gather information and write your portion of a personal ad to go in their national members resource book. Today you will research and write a section of the ad describing Satan's personality. First research your group's information, then write that section of the ad on the "Personal Ad Final Input Sheet."

This is where you will find the real heart of the client's personality. Do your research, keeping track of those key personality traits that make a personality profile come alive.

Matthew 4:1-10 ....

John 8:44 ....

2 Corinthians 4:4 ....

2 Corinthians 11:14 ....

Ephesians 2:2 ....

1 Timothy 4:1 ....

James 2:19 ....

1 Peter 5:8 ....

Revelation 12:10 ....

Complete the following sentence and write a paragraph using the information you have researched.
Personal Ad Final Input Sheet
Client: Satan
Group Three: Satan's Personality Profile
Hi!, I'm Satan and I am... ....

....

....

....

....

....

....

....

....

THE
PROFILE OF THE
ENEMY

Group Four: Satan's Activities and Hobbies

You are on the staff of a nationally-known companionship company called "Equally Stoked" that links personalities together based on their origins, personality traits, activities and hobbies. Your job is to gather information and write your portion of a personal ad to go in their national members resource book. Today you will research and write a section for the ad about Satan's activities and hobbies. First research your group's information, then write that section of the ad on the "Personal Ad Final Input Sheet."

Who the enemy is dictates what the enemy does. Using the verses below identify 11 traits of the enemy. From those traits identify two specific ways you've seen evidence of the enemy's activity in the world you live in.

	Trait of the enemy	Evidence
Matthew 4:1		
John 8:44		
2 Corinthians 4:4		
2 Corinthians 11:14		
Ephesians 2:2		
1 Timothy 4:1		
James 2:19		
1 Peter 5:8		
Revelation 12:10		

Complete the following sentence and write a paragraph using the information you have researched.
Personal Ad Final Input Sheet
Client: Satan
Group Four: Satan's Activities and Hobbies
Hi!, I'm Satan and I spend my time...

So What?

1. What new information did you learn about the enemy?

....

....

2. What are two reasons why you wouldn't respond to the enemy's "Equally Stoked" ad?

....

....

How do these sins relate to the words of Jesus in Matthew 6:19-24?

....

....

3. Why do so few people treasure that which moths or thieves cannot destroy or steal?

....

....

What does that phrase mean and how can you apply it to your spiritual life?

....

....

Things to Think About

1. Where did the devil come from?

....

....

2. If you were to describe the enemy with several one-word descriptions, what words would you use and why?

....

....

3. What are some ways you can keep Satan from being your friend?

....

....

....

THE
PROFILE OF THE
ENEMY

PARENT PAGE

SATAN CAME FROM WHERE?

Interview each other using the following questions:

1. How would you describe Satan?

2. Where do you think Satan came from originally?

3. What is evidence of Satan's work in the world that you have seen?

4. If God were to get in a fight with the enemy, who would win and why?

5. John 8:44 gives a very clear description of how Jesus saw Satan. What words does Jesus use to describe the enemy?

6. What can believers do to keep the enemy from messing up their lives?

Pray for one another's protection from the enemy's schemes.

Session 6 "The Profile of the Enemy"
Date

THE GOALS AND WEAPONS OF THE ENEMY

K EY VERSES

"'The thief comes only to steal and kill and destroy; I have come that they may have life and have it to the full.'" John 10:10

B IBLICAL BASIS

Genesis 2:16; 3:2-5,13;
Psalm 18:29;
Matthew 4:1-11; 12:43-45;
16:21-23; 24:23,24;
Mark 5:2-8;
Luke 10:17;
John 8:3-11,43,44; 10:10; 15:19;
Acts 19:13-16;
Romans 1:25;
1 Corinthians 10:12,13;
2 Corinthians 2:5-11; 4:4; 10:3-5;
Galatians 3:26;
Ephesians 4:25-32; 6:12;
1 Timothy 4:1,2; 6:9,10;
2 Timothy 1:5;
James 1:13-16; 4:1-12;
2 Peter 2:4;
1 John 3:7-10;
Revelation 9:2-21; 12:9,10,14;
16:13,14

T HE BIG IDEA

We can keep the enemy's deceit from becoming our defeat when we know the plans and tools he and his team use to conquer God's children.

A IMS OF THIS SESSION

During this session you will guide students to:

- Examine the weapons the enemy uses to conquer a Christian's faith;
- Discover the effects of those weapons on a believer's life;
- Implement a defensive strategy against the enemy's work in their lives.

W ARM UP

COMPARISONS—

An activity to discuss descriptions of Satan.

T EAM EFFORT— JUNIOR HIGH/ MIDDLE SCHOOL

GUMMY BEAR TOWER—

Students work together to build a tower.

T EAM EFFORT— HIGH SCHOOL

MEET JANET—

A case study that challenges students to share God's love and truth with a nonbeliever.

I N THE WORD

BEGINNING MOUNTAIN CLIMBING 101—

A Bible study on the methods and purposes of Satan.

T HINGS TO THINK ABOUT (OPTIONAL)

Questions to get students thinking and talking about how Satan tries to deceive Christians.

P ARENT PAGE

A tool to get the session into the home and allow parents and young people to discuss any generational footholds that Satan may be using against their family.

THE GOALS AND WEAPONS OF THE ENEMY

LEADER'S DEVOTIONAL

"With your help I can advance against a troop; with my God I can scale a wall" (Psalm 18:29).

Taking on a mountain is a dangerous task—one not to be taken lightly. Rock climbing and hiking are two of my favorite activities, yet there have been plenty of times when I've been humbled by the sheer size, height and power of certain mountains I've attempted to climb. Do you want a few lessons in humility? There was the time two friends of mine and I spent the night tied to the face of a thousand-foot rock only a hundred feet short of reaching the summit—without flashlights! Climbing by starlight just doesn't cut it. Or what about the time our climbing party got stopped short at 14,000 feet by wind and hail on Mt. Whitney. Or the time I took four successive twenty-foot falls on a blasted rock face called Suicide Mountains. All of these experiences were wonderful instructors in humility.

The Christian life is often compared to a long journey marked by dangerous passes, difficult climbs and safe stretches of peaceful pasture. Scripture warns us that Satan lurks along the road of our journey using any tool, roadblock or pothole to distract us on our way. He will use any temptation, thought, event or circumstance to trip us up. This lesson will equip both you and your students to understand how Satan wants to destroy your relationship with God. He will use your weaknesses, your regrets of the past, guilt, lies or any other dirty trick to cause you to fall away from Christ. Whether fear, fatigue or loneliness, Satan has a scheme and a strategy for each one of us. Though at times we may face difficult struggles and disappointing setbacks as disillusionment sets in, we must remind ourselves who we are in Christ and God's promises of victory for us. God uses the setbacks we encounter to humble us and cause us to depend on Him. He uses the tests we experience to reaffirm His commitment to us as our heavenly Father.

God promises to protect us from all evil as we walk through the valley of the shadow of death. We do not walk alone. It's easy to forget Jesus' presence when we are distracted by the busy lives that we lead. Our schedules often crowd God out of our lives, and before long, we feel lost and alone like sheep without a shepherd. Satan wants you to be and most of all, feel isolated from the presence of God. Believe it or not, you can feel alone and isolated even in the midst of leading a busy life filled with ministry and caring for the needs of others.

Thank God that we can call on Him at any moment to receive help in our time of need. God wants you to first enjoy His presence and experience His peace in your life. When we get too busy in ministry, that truth is easy to forget. Before you prepare for this lesson, spend some time alone with God thanking Him for His constant presence in your life. Remember you are not alone; Jesus is with you every step of the way. (Written by Joey O'Connor.)

"The devil is a better theologian than any of us and is a devil still."—A. W. Tozer

THE GOALS AND WEAPONS OF THE ENEMY

KEY VERSES

"The thief comes only to steal and kill and destroy; I have come that they may have life and have it to the full." John 10:10

BIBLICAL BASIS

Genesis 2:16; 3:2-5,13; Psalm 18:29; Matthew 4:1-11; 12:43-45; 16:21-23; 24:23,24; Mark 5:2-8; Luke 10:17; John 8:3-11, 43,44; 10:10; 15:19; Acts 19:13-16; Romans 1:25; 1 Corinthians 10:12,13; 2 Corinthians 2:5-11; 4:4; 10:35; Galatians 3:26; Ephesians 4:25-32; 6:12; 1 Timothy 4:1,2; 6:9,10; 2 Timothy 1:5; James 1:13-16; 4:1-12; 2 Peter 2:4; 1 John 3:7-10; Revelation 9:2-21; 12:9,10,14; 16:13,14

THE BIG IDEA

We can keep the enemy's deceit from becoming our defeat when we know the plans and tools he and his team use to conquer God's children.

WARM UP (5-10 MINUTES)

COMPARISONS

• From the word pairs below have the students choose the word they think best describes Satan and explain why they think so.
Is Satan more like...

a tornado	or	an earthquake?
a chameleon	or	a panther?
a Wiffle ball	or	a marshmallow?
a zipper	or	Velcro?
M&Ms	or	Spam?
fire	or	water?

1 John 3:7-10
What are some other natural footholds that you see in the lives of people?

Team Six: Climbing Ropes—Schemes
Read 2 Corinthians 2:5-11 and see if you can identify a potential scheme Satan may be able to use to conquer a Christian.

What is the ultimate outcome when believers don't forgive someone who has hurt them?

Read Matthew 4:1-11 to see how Satan was trying to force wedges and clips into Jesus' weaknesses for attaching his (Satan's) own rope. What ultimate scheme do you think the devil was attempting to rope Jesus into?

SO WHAT?

1. Why do you think the enemy goes to so much trouble to get a believer's attention away from God?

2. Thinking back over what you've learned, identify one scheme the enemy is using to rope you into moving in his direction.

3. What are two footholds you have allowed to remain in your life which the enemy easily uses to draw you away from God's best?

What can you do to remove these footholds from your life?

THINGS TO THINK ABOUT (OPTIONAL)

• Use the questions on page 89 after or as part of "In the Word."
1. How can we know that there is an enemy who stands in opposition to God?

2. What are the tools that the enemy uses to conquer Christians?

3. How have you seen the enemy successfully lure a believer away from a growing relationship with Jesus?

PARENT PAGE

• Distribute page to parents.

TEAM EFFORT—JUNIOR HIGH/
MIDDLE SCHOOL (15-20 MINUTES)

GUMMY BEAR TOWER

- Divide students into teams of four to six. Give each group 30 gummy bears and several toothpicks. The object of the game is to build the highest free-standing tower using the gummy bears as strongholds and the toothpicks as cross supports.
- Give the groups about 10 minutes to build their towers. Call time and measure the height of each tower. The winning team is the one who has the highest tower still standing when time is up.
- Discuss the following questions:
  1. What made this game difficult?
  2. What held the toothpicks together?
  3. In Ephesians 4:27, Paul tells believers: "Do not give the devil a foothold." Satan uses "footholds and strongholds" to build a tower against God's work in our lives. The footholds and strongholds are the sins, lies, thoughts, etc. that take us away from God. What are some footholds and strongholds that Christians struggle with?

TEAM EFFORT—HIGH SCHOOL (15-20 MINUTES)

MEET JANET

- Divide students into groups of three or four.
- Read the case study on page 89 to the whole group.
- Have the small groups discuss what they would tell Janet.
- If time allows, have some of the groups—or individuals—role-play what they would tell Janet.

What would you say?

IN THE WORD (25-30 MINUTES)

BEGINNING MOUNTAIN CLIMBING 101

- Give each student a copy of "In the Word" on pages 83-89 and a pen or pencil.
- Complete sections I and II with the whole group.
- Then divide students into six groups.
- From section III, assign each group one of the six team reports.
- Allow time at the end of the study for each group to give its report.

I. SATAN'S MOUNTAIN TO CLIMB—MOUNT CHRISTIAN
A. What do these passages say that make Mount Christian an intriguing climb for the enemy?

John 15:19 _____

Galatians 3:26 _____

B. What do these passages say Satan's goal is for conquering Mount Christian?

John 10:10 _____

1 Timothy 4:1-2 _____

Revelation 12:9 _____

II. SATAN'S CLIMBING PARTNERS—DEMONS
A. Scripture refers to four different ranks of demons.
B. Read the following verses about demons, then answer the questions: Matthew 12:43-45; Mark 5:2-8; Luke 10:17; Acts 19:13-16; Ephesians 6:12; Revelation 16:13,14

III. SATAN'S BAG OF CLIMBING TOOLS
Team One: A Climber's Hammer—Deceptions

Genesis 2:16; 3:2-5,13 _____

Matthew 24:23,24 _____

John 8:43,44 _____

Romans 1:25 _____

2 Corinthians 4:4 _____

Team Two: The Climber's Pick—Accusations

Revelation 12:10 _____

John 8:3-11 (How is the accuser at work in this story?)

_____

James 4:7,8,11,12 _____

Team Three: Climbing Wedges—Strongholds
1. Read 2 Corinthians 10:3-5. Define a climbing wedge or a stronghold in your own words.

_____

2. If a stronghold has to do with planted thoughts that go against God's truths, then in Matthew 16:21-23 what evidence of a stronghold do we see in the encounter between Christ and Peter?

_____

3. A common stronghold with which both believers and nonbelievers struggle is the thought that God the Father could never forgive them for what they have done. This can keep them from trusting God for their future, not allowing His love to fill them and to become real to them thus, affecting their ability to forgive others. What are some other common climbing wedges, or strongholds, that you see or hear friends talk about that are contrary to the truths of God our heavenly Father?

Team Four: Climbing Clips—Temptation

1 Corinthians 10:12,13 _____

1 Timothy 6:9,10 _____

James 1:13-16 _____

Team Five: Natural Footholds—Our Sin Nature

James 4:1-12 _____

Fold

 **N THE WORD**

BEGINNING MOUNTAIN CLIMBING 101

In this session you will learn the basics of mountain climbing through studying the climbing strategies of an expert in conquering mountains—Satan. In order to begin, we must understand some basic "must-haves" for a successful climb.

A climber must have…

1. A mountain with many natural footholds.
2. A climbing goal.
3. A climbing partner or partners.
4. A bag of climbing tools: hammer, pick, clips, wedges and ropes.

As you go through the session outline step-by-step, you will study Satan's familiar climb of "Mount Christian." As you study the techniques of this crafty climber, look closely at how he uses his tools to conquer Mount Christian. Keep in mind that believers are the mountains that Satan tries to conquer everyday.

I. Satan's Mountain to Climb—Mount Christian

A. What do these passages say that make Mount Christian an intriguing climb for the enemy?

John 15:19 ....

....

Galatians 3:26 ....

....

B. What do these passages say Satan's goal is for conquering Mount Christian?

John 10:10 ....

....

1 Timothy 4:1-2 ....

....

Revelation 12:9 ....

....

II. Satan's Climbing Partners—Demons

A. Scripture refers to four different ranks of demons.
1. Rebellious angels bound and cast into the abyss, or pit (see Revelation 9:2-12).
2. Fallen angels so wicked that they've been bound in hell until judgment (see 2 Peter 2:4).
3. Four evil angels bound within the earth at the river Euphrates (see Revelation 9:13-21).
4. Satan's usual climbing partners are earth-dwelling demons (see Matthew 12:43-45 and Ephesians 6:12).

**THE GOALS AND
WEAPONS OF THE
ENEMY**

IN THE WORD

B. Read the following verses about demons, then answer the questions: Matthew 12:43-45; Mark 5:2-8; Luke 10:17; Acts 19:13-16; Ephesians 6:12; Revelation 16:13,14

I. What can demons do?

2. What can't they do?

3. What do they know?

4. Who do they serve?

III. Satan's Bag of Climbing Tools

To better understand each of Satan's "climbing tools," your team will report to the whole group about your team's "tool" by reading the following verses and answering the questions.

Team One: A Climber's Hammer—Deceptions

A climber's hammer is used to pound away at the rock to remove debris, to make hand- or footholds or to drive wedges deep into the stone to create a more climbable and controllable surface.

After reading the verses below, describe how Satan uses the hammer of deception to drive lies deep into the mind of Mount Christian and what the results are.

Genesis 2;16; 3:2-5,13

Matthew 24:23,24

John 8:43,44

Romans 1:25

2 Corinthians 4:4

Report Questions:

I. What is this tool used for?

IN THE WORD

2. How does Satan use the tool in conquering Mount Christian?

....

....

3. What are some obvious deceptions believers struggle with daily?

....

....

Team Two: The Climber's Pick—Accusations
With the climber's pick the climber digs at cracks in the rock to better place the climbing wedges to aid in climbing through difficult areas.

After reading the following verses, describe how Satan uses the pick of accusation to drive thoughts into believers' heads and what the results of these accusations are.

Revelation 12:10 ....

....

John 8:3-11 (How is the accuser at work in this story?) ....

....

James 4:7,8,11,12 ....

....

Report Questions:

1. What is this tool used for?

....

....

2. How does Satan use the tool in conquering Mount Christian?

....

....

3. What are some common accusations believers struggle with on a daily basis?

....

....

Team Three: Climbing Wedges—Strongholds
Climbing wedges are used to create strongholds in the crevices and weak spots of the rock. The climber may use his climbing pick to create a crack just large enough to hammer in a climbing wedge. Onto these wedges the climber attaches his climbing clips giving him a solid stronghold to conquer the difficult areas of the mountain where there are no natural footholds.

THE GOALS AND WEAPONS OF THE ENEMY

IN THE WORD

1. Read 2 Corinthians 10:3-5. Define a climbing wedge or a stronghold in your own words.

    ....

    ....

2. If a stronghold has to do with planted thoughts that go against God's truths, then in Matthew 16:21-23 what evidence of a stronghold do we see in the encounter between Christ and Peter?

    ....

    ....

3. A common stronghold with which both believers and nonbelievers struggle is the thought that God the Father could never forgive them for what they have done. This can keep them from trusting God for their future, not allowing His love to fill them and to become real to them thus, affecting their ability to forgive others. What are some other common climbing wedges, or strongholds, that you see or hear friends talk about that are contrary to the truths of God our heavenly Father?

    ....

    ....

Report Questions:

1. What is this tool used for?

    ....

    ....

2. How does Satan use the tool in conquering Mount Christian?

    ....

    ....

3. What are some common strongholds Satan has placed into the crevices of believers' lives?

    ....

    ....

Team Four: Climbing Clips—Temptation

With a climbing clip a climber is able to attach himself to the face of the rock. Through these clips he threads his climbing rope, securing himself and his tool bag to the face of the mountain.

Using the following verses, describe how the enemy uses the climbing clips of temptation to grab our attention and report what the effects of temptation are:

1 Corinthians 10:12,13 ....

1 Timothy 6:9,10 ....

James 1:13-16 ....

....

Report Questions:

1. What is this tool used for?

....

2. How does Satan use this tool in conquering Mount Christian?

....

3. What are some common temptations believers struggle with?

....

....

Team Five: Natural Footholds—Our Sin Nature

There are natural footholds on the face of a mountain that make it easy for climbers to scale the mountain they're conquering. These are easy for the climber to find because the footholds have been a part of the rock for generations.

From the following passages, identify some specific footholds used by the enemy and what the consequences to the believer are:

James 4:1-12 ....

....

1 John 3:7-10 ....

....

Pride, greed and inappropriate expressions of anger are some examples of natural footholds that the enemy uses to get a good grip on believers. There may also be even larger and deeper generational footholds such as alcoholism and abuse that make it even easier for Satan to scale Mount Christian. What are some other natural footholds that you see in the lives of people?

....

Report Questions:

1. What is this tool used for?

....

2. How does Satan use this tool in conquering Mount Christian?

....

3. What are some natural footholds common to believers' lives that make it easy for Satan to climb and conquer?

....

....

THE GOALS AND WEAPONS OF THE ENEMY

IN THE WORD

Team Six: Climbing Ropes—Schemes

A climber is able to secure himself to the mountain by threading his climbing rope through the clips, which are attached to the wedges that are jammed into the crevices. Satan conquers Mount Christian in the same way.

Read 2 Corinthians 2:5-11 and see if you can identify a potential scheme Satan may be able to use to conquer a Christian.

....

....

What is the ultimate outcome when believers don't forgive someone who has hurt them?

....

....

Read Matthew 4:1-11 to see how Satan was trying to attach his rope by forcing wedges and clips into Jesus' weaknesses. What ultimate scheme do you think the devil was attempting to rope Jesus into?

....

....

Report Questions:

1. What is this tool used for?

....

....

2. How does Satan use this tool in conquering Mount Christian?

....

....

3. What are some common schemes Satan uses to tangle up Christians and make them conquerable?

....

....

SO WHAT?

1. Why do you think the enemy goes to so much trouble to get a believer's attention away from God?

....

....

....

2. Thinking back over what you've learned, identify one scheme the enemy is using to rope you into moving in his direction.

....

....

....

3. What are two footholds you have allowed to remain in your life which the enemy easily uses to draw you away from God's best?

....

....

What can you do to remove these footholds from your life?

....

....

Things to Think About

1. How can we know that there is an enemy who stands in opposition to God?

....

....

2. What do you think are some of the tools the enemy uses to drag Christians away from God's best?

....

....

3. How have you seen the enemy successfully lure another believer away from a growing relationship with Jesus?

....

....

Team Effort

MEET JANET

Janet is a fifteen-year-old girl whose looks tell anyone she has lived a tough life. Behind the hairstyle, clothes and jewelry is the face of a sweet young girl whose appearance and lifestyle says "Don't come to close."

The first words from her mouth are "I don't believe there is a God and I don't believe there is a heaven. I do believe there is a hell and a devil and I can't wait to spend eternity with him."

Further conversations with her reveal that throughout her life she has felt rejected. A large part of the rejection has been reinforced by the abuses she has experienced while growing up. You find out that she has had experiences with gang activity, drug use, suicide attempts and multiple stays in drug rehabilitation clinics. It is clear she does not understand the dynamics of the spiritual battle, she cannot comprehend a God of love because she has never experienced love.

She now sits before you allowing you to get close enough to her to be able to share about the God you know. What would you say?

**THE GOALS AND
WEAPONS OF THE
ENEMY**

⬤ᴘᴀʀᴇɴᴛ ᴘᴀɢᴇ

HAND-ME-DOWNS

1. Read 2 Timothy 1:5 together. Paul writes about Timothy's "hand-me-down faith." Who passed their faith on to Timothy?

   ....

   ....

   ....

2. We pick up many positive and negative traits from our parents. Share with each other some positive and negative traits that were passed on to you.

   ....

   ....

   ....

3. Paul identifies Timothy's faith as being a godly hand-me-down. What are some godly hand-me-downs in your family?

   ....

   ....

   ....

4. Just as there are godly traits passed down, there are also generational footholds or sins. Read Ephesians 4:25-32 to define a foothold. What are some of the footholds listed in this passage?

   ....

   ....

We know that alcoholism, insecurities and abuse are generational footholds. Share with each other some hand-me-down footholds knowing that confession is the beginning of winning the battle.

Pray for each other's victory over these hand-me-down footholds.

Session 7 "The Goals and Weapons of the Enemy" Date ....

UPROOTING THE ENEMY'S SCHEMES

KEY VERSES

"Test everything. Hold on to the good. Avoid every kind of evil."
1 Thessalonians 5:21,22

BIBLICAL BASIS

Matthew 13:24-30;
John 8:31,32;
Romans 8:13,14; 12:2;
Philippians 4:6-8;
Colossians 2:8;
1 Thessalonians 5:21,22;
James 3:7-12

THE BIG IDEA

We can identify and defend against the attacks of the enemy by testing every spirit.

AIMS OF THIS SESSION

During this session you will guide students to:
• Examine their lives for evidence of the enemy's attacks;
• Discover how to weed the lies of the enemy from their lives;
• Implement a self-defense and deweeding strategy.

WARM UP

ONE THING LEADS TO ANOTHER—

Students see how thoughts lead to feelings that lead to actions.

TEAM EFFORT— JUNIOR HIGH/ MIDDLE SCHOOL

PROTECT YOUR SPACE—

A game related to protecting the Christian life from Satan's schemes.

TEAM EFFORT— HIGH SCHOOL

IDENTIFY THE LIE—

Students examine a case study for examples of how the enemy lies to nonbelievers.

IN THE WORD

FARMERS, FLOWERS AND WEEDS—

A Bible study on how to weed out the bad influences and encourage the good ones in the Christian life.

THINGS TO THINK ABOUT (OPTIONAL)

Questions to get the students thinking and talking about how to grow stronger in their relationship with God.

PARENT PAGE

A tool to get the session into the home and allow parents and young people to discuss how to break bad habits and develop good ones.

UPROOTING THE ENEMY'S SCHEMES

LEADER'S DEVOTIONAL

"See to it that no one takes you captive through hollow and deceptive philosophy, which depends on human tradition and the basic principles of this world rather than on Christ" (Colossians 2:8).

When my brother was in the U.S. Navy, one of his principle duties was working in the Command Intelligence Center, commonly referred to as the CIC. The CIC is the place on all Navy warships where both friend and foe are tracked by sophisticated radar. The main purpose of the CIC is to protect the ship from incoming attacks. Using elaborate high-tech equipment, the people who work in the CIC are able to track the movement and activity of ships, planes and submarines from hundreds of miles away. The CIC is the first line of defense to warn the ship's crew of any incoming missiles or torpedoes. In times of war, the reliability of the CIC could mean the difference between life and death.

As Christians, God has given us our own Command Intelligence Center. Our CIC is the Holy Spirit at work in us—the spiritual radar we use to detect the oncoming attacks of Satan. The Holy Spirit guides our thoughts, motives and attitudes by transforming our mind with the mind of Christ. Because of God's power within us, we are able to discern and test every thought. The more we grow in the knowledge of God's word, the more we can fill our minds with His truth in order to discover how He wants us to live.

Our minds are the seedbeds of our actions. If Satan can fill our minds with negative thoughts, destructive thinking and guilt-filled anxiety, then His work will soon influence our actions. If we harbor jealousy, envy, lust, doubt, hatred, bitterness or any other secret sin in the dark hidden corners of our minds, it is only a little while before our lives will produce the fruit of our flesh. By understanding how Satan tries to attack our minds with his lies and deceit, then we can use the power of God's word to develop a defense system that Satan will never be able to penetrate.

What areas of your mind are most vulnerable to Satan's attacks? How are you filling your mind with God's word? How has God's word helped you to discern the fiery lies of your enemy? In what way can you rely on God to protect you from Satan's influence? How does our culture impact your thoughts, feelings and attitudes? Think about these questions as you prepare this lesson. Fill your mind with the presence of God as you seek to impact the lives of young people for eternity. No matter what the enemy attempts to do in your life, you are a son or daughter of the King. Jesus Christ's death and resurrection sealed the defeat of Satan and we can rest assured in the hope of our salvation. (Written by Joey O'Connor.)

**Sin has many tools, but a lie is the handle that fits them all.
—Anonymous**

UPROOTING THE ENEMY'S SCHEMES

KEY VERSES

"Test everything. Hold on to the good. Avoid every kind of evil." 1 Thessalonians 5:21,22

BIBLICAL BASIS

Matthew 13:24-30; John 8:31,32; Romans 8:13,14; 12:2; Philippians 4:6-8; Colossians 2:8; 1 Thessalonians 5:21,22; James 3:7-12

THE BIG IDEA

We can identify and defend against the attacks of the enemy by testing every spirit.

WARM UP (5-10 MINUTES)

ONE THING LEADS TO ANOTHER

• Have students form pairs.
• Give each student a copy of "One Thing Leads to Another" on page 95, or display a copy using an overhead projector.
• Read the following statements and have the students complete them aloud in their pairs:

Share your completions of the following statements with your partner.

When I think of the first day of school, I feel .... and it makes me want to ....

When I think of my best friend, I feel .... and it makes me want to ....

When I think of my worst enemy, I feel .... and it makes me want to ....

When I think of falling in love, I feel .... and it makes me want to ....

When I think of the struggles I face, I feel .... and it makes me want to ....

Fold

---

1. What is a situation or struggle you are going through or have gone through, that has left you feeling hurt, angry, resentful, anxious, frustrated, sad, depressed, etc.?

2. What specific feelings does that struggle leave you with? (It is important to list as many feelings as you can identify.)

3. Have you felt those feelings before? Write down a struggle in your past when you felt those same feelings. What are some of those feelings you felt during that past situation?

4. What was your reaction or acting out behavior? (Include your actions, thoughts and attitudes. For example: anger, isolation, resentment, revenge, rebellion, submissiveness, performance behavior, attention-getting methods, wanting to prove them wrong, some form of denial, any other self-defeating behavior.)

5. What deception is/was involved in your reaction, thoughts or attitudes? (Examples: I can't do anything right; I can't trust anyone; no one really loves me; the only safe thing to do is escape; they'll be sorry when...; I am worthless.)

6. What biblical truth or truths can you plant in the place of the weed as you pull it from your field?

7. Write a prayer to Jesus committing this transformation to Him and asking Him to guide you as you get used to planting new flowers in your field.

THINGS TO THINK ABOUT (OPTIONAL)

• Use the questions on page 100 after or as part of "In the Word."
1. There are three types of things in our lives that affect our relationship with God.
   What are some things that help us grow stronger in our relationship with God?

   What are some things that keep us from growing in our relationship with God?

   What are some things that cause us to grow weaker in our relationship with God?

2. How do you determine which things help you grow stronger and which do not?

3. How does a person change a "growing-weaker" behavior into a "growing-stronger" behavior?

PARENT PAGE

• Distribute page to parents.

PROTECT YOUR SPACE

- Divide students into four groups.
- You will need to provide a ping pong ball and a round or square table. Have spare ping pong balls in case of accidents. The table top should be marked off into four equal sections with a masking tape X.
- The object of the game is to not allow the ball to be blown off the edge in your own space while trying to blow the ball off the edge of someone else's space.
- A member from each team must kneel near the edge of the table in front of his or her team's space only. The players must be back from the tables with hands clasped behind their backs.
- Place the ping pong ball in the center of the table. On go, the teams blow until the ball falls off the edge of a team's space. The team who has the ball fall off its side gets a point. The team that has the least points at the end of the game is the winner. You may not block the ball with anything but air.
- Have the next member of each team kneel at the table. Continue play as long as time allows or until everyone has played at least once.
- Discuss the following questions:
  1. What were you asked to protect?
  2. What made it hard to protect your space?
  3. In life we play protect-your-space except it's not from a ping pong ball. What are some things Christians need to protect their space from?

IDENTIFY THE LIE

- Divide students into groups of three or four.
- Give each group a copy of "Identify the Lie" on page 96.
- Have each group read and discuss the story.
- If time allows, have the groups share their answers to the last question with the whole group.

Discuss the following:

What are the lies in Jackie's story?

What specific occurrences do you think have fed the lies the most?

If Jackie asked you for help, what would you tell her?

IN THE WORD (25-30 MINUTES)

FARMERS, FLOWERS AND WEEDS

- Divide students into groups of three or four.
- Give each student a copy of "In the Word" on pages 97-99 and a pen or pencil, or display a copy using an overhead projector.

--- Fold ---

- Have students complete the Bible study.

1. Your life is like the parable of the farmer. In your case the field is your life and you are the farmer. The parable says you have two things growing in your field, what are they?

....

2. Where did the weeds come from?

....

3. The parable implies that flowers are the good things which make people better, and weeds are the bad things which make people bitter.
   What are two flowers you have in your field?

   What are two weeds you have in your field?

....

4. As the farmer of your own field, answer the questions below.

   | What are five things a farmer can do to grow good flowers?
 i.e. Talk positively | What are five things a farmer can do to kill good flowers?
 i.e. Talk negatively |

5. As the farmer of your life, answer the questions below using the answers above as guidelines.

   | What are five things we can do to grow a good life?
 i.e. Hang out with affirming people | What are five things we can do to kill a good life?
 i.e. Hang out with mean people |

....

6. What does 1 Thessalonians 5:21,22 tell believers they must do with the things growing in their field to produce a fruitful life?

....

7. Why does Romans 12:2 say believers are to test the things growing in their field?

....

8. What will the results of testing your life for flowers and weeds be?

....

SO WHAT?
THE WEED-BE-GONE TEST

Once the enemy has sown weeds into our field, we need to be able get them out. It is Christ's desire to set us free from all our weeds (see John 8:31,32). This worksheet is a tool you can use to weed the enemy's deceptions from your life. Follow it step-by-step and learn to take out the weeds and put flowers in their place.

WARM UP

ONE THING LEADS TO ANOTHER

Share your completions of the following statements with your partner.

When I think of the first day of school, I feel .... and it makes me want to

....

When I think of my best friend, I feel .... and it makes me want to

....

When I think of my worst enemy, I feel .... and it makes me want to

....

When I think of falling in love, I feel.. and it makes me want to

....

When I think of the struggles I face, I feel .... and it makes me want to

....

UPROOTING
THE ENEMY'S
SCHEMES

TEAM EFFORT

IDENTIFY THE LIE

Her name is Jackie and she believes that God is a self-centered control freak. Jackie feels that God created people to be played with like chess pieces on a chessboard.

Jackie didn't just wake up one day and decide this. She is a victim of a scheme that has left her doubting the existence of God or at least doubting that He is a loving God.

Here is the rest of Jackie's story. It is your job to identify the untruth in her testimony and see if you can figure out how she came to the conclusion that she did.

Jackie was born into an alcoholic family. Her dad abandoned the family when she was six years old. He didn't come back into the picture until Jackie was about ten. When he returned, he tried to reestablish a relationship with Jackie, but her mom didn't trust him so she wouldn't allow it. Finally, her mom slowly let Jackie's dad back into her life.

When Jackie turned 12 years old, her dad sexually abused her and then disappeared again. At 14, Jackie had a relationship with an older teenager that became sexual as well. After about a month, he left her brokenhearted.

Jackie has a warped sense of reality. She is searching for the love she never got from her dad in the relationships she builds with guys, but she is unhappy, hopeless and hurting. Jackie believes that if God had never made her, she wouldn't have been molested. She believes ultimately the mess that her life has become is all God's fault.

Discuss the following questions:

What are the lies in Jackie's story?

What specific occurrences do you think have fed the lies the most?

If Jackie asked you for help, what would you tell her?

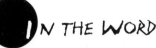 IN THE WORD

FARMERS, FLOWERS AND WEEDS

Write your name in the blanks of the parable below. Read it aloud as a group with each member verbalizing his or her name in the appropriate places.

The kingdom of heaven is like a farmer named .... who sowed good seed in his (or her) field. But while everyone was sleeping, ...'s enemy came and sowed weeds among the flowers and went away. When the flowers sprouted and formed buds, the weeds also appeared.

.............................'s servants came to him (or her) and said, "..............................., didn't you sow good seed in your field? Where then did the weeds come from?"

"An enemy did this," .... replied.

The servants asked him, "Do you want us to go and pull them up?"

"No," .... answered, "because while you are pulling the weeds, you may uproot the flowers with them. Let both grow together until the harvest. At that time I will tell the harvesters: First, collect the weeds and tie them in bundles to be burned; then gather the flowers and bring them into my warehouse" (a paraphrase of Matthew 13:24-30).

1. Your life is like the parable of the farmer. In your case the field is your life and you are the farmer. The parable says you have two things growing in your field, what are they?

   ....

   ....

2. Where did the weeds come from?

   ....

   ....

3. The parable implies that flowers are the good things which make people better, and weeds are the bad things which make people bitter.

   What are two flowers you have in your field? ....

   What are two weeds you have in your field? ....

4. As the farmer of your own field, answer the questions below.

What are five things a farmer can do to grow good flowers? i.e. Talk positively	What are five things a farmer can do to kill good flowers? i.e. Talk negatively
....	....
....	....
....	....
....	....
....	....

UPROOTING THE ENEMY'S SCHEMES

IN THE WORD

5. As the farmer of your life, answer the questions below using the answers above as guidelines.

What are five things we can do to grow a good life? i.e. Hang out with affirming people	What are five things we can do to kill a good life? i.e. Hang out with mean people

6. What does 1 Thessalonians 5:21,22 tell believers they must do with the things growing in their field to produce a fruitful life?

7. Why does Romans 12:2 say believers are to test the things growing in their field?

8. What will be the results of testing your life for flowers and weeds?

SO WHAT?
The Weed-Be-Gone Test

Once the enemy has sown weeds into our field, we need to be able get them out.

It is Christ's desire to set us free from all our weeds (see John 8:31,32). This worksheet is a tool you can use to weed the enemy's deceptions from your life. Follow it step-by-step and learn to take out the weeds and put flowers in their places.

1. What is a situation or struggle you are going through or have gone through, that has left you feeling hurt, angry, resentful, anxious, frustrated, sad, depressed, etc.?

2. What specific feelings does that struggle leave you with? (It is important to list as many feelings as you can identify.)

3. Have you felt those feelings before? Write down a struggle in your past when you felt those same feelings. What are some of those feelings you felt during that past situation?

 N THE WORD

4. What was your reaction or acting out behavior during this past situation? (Include your actions, thoughts and attitudes. For example: anger, isolation, resentment, revenge, rebellion, submissiveness, performance behavior, attention-getting methods, wanting to prove them wrong, some form of denial, any other self-defeating behavior.)

....

....

....

5. What deception was involved in your reaction, thoughts or attitudes? (Examples: I can't do anything right; I can't trust anyone; no one really loves me; the only safe thing to do is escape; they'll be sorry when...; I am worthless.)

....

....

....

6. What biblical truth or truths can you plant in the place of the weed as you pull it from your field?

....

....

....

7. Write a prayer to Jesus committing this transformation to Him and asking Him to guide you as you get used to planting new flowers in your field.

....

....

....

UPROOTING THE ENEMY'S SCHEMES

Things to Think About

1. There are three types of things in our lives that affect our relationship with God.

   What are some things that help us grow stronger in our relationship with God?

   ....

   ....

   What are some things that keep us from growing in our relationship with God?

   ....

   ....

   ....

   What are some things that cause us to grow weaker in our relationship with God?

   ....

   ....

2. **How do you determine which things help you grow stronger and which do not?**

   ....

   ....

   ....

3. **How does a person change a "growing-weaker" behavior into a "growing-stronger" behavior?**

   ....

   ....

   ....

PARENT PAGE

BUILDING BETTER BEHAVIORS

Viewers sat with their eyes glued to the television set in astonishment as an 8,000 pound elephant used its trunk to swing a beautiful Hollywood actress around in circles by her leg and flip her up onto its back. It was all happening on Hollywood's "Circus of the Stars." Here is this huge animal with enough strength to crush the huskiest woman or for that matter miscalculate the flip onto its back and accidentally flip her over its shoulder into the upper level seating in the big top. Much to many viewers' amazement, and perhaps disappointment, that didn't happen.

Read James 3:7-12.

1. What is James right about in verse 7?

....

....

....

2. What does James say that is also true in verse 8?

....

....

....

3. James doesn't come out and say it, but if we can't tame the tongue, who can?

....

....

....

4. In our own strength old habits are hard to break and new habits are hard to learn, but there is hope. How does Paul say we can form new habits in Romans 8:13,14?

....

....

....

5. According to the Romans passage, who gives us the strength to break our habits?

....

....

....

Session 8 "Uprooting the Enemy's Schemes"
Date ....

PARENT PAGE

6. Often some of our habits don't make us better people for God. Instead, they make us bitter people. Share with each other two bitterness-building behaviors that you need to stop doing.

    ....

    ....

    ....

7. What does Philippians 4:8 say we're to put in place of the old behaviors?

    ....

    ....

    ....

8. What are two better behaviors you will put in place of the old bitter ones?

    ....

    ....

    ....

Pray for each other concerning these decisions.

Unit III

PUTTING ON GOD'S ARMOR

LEADER'S PEP TALK

By the time this book gets into your hands, another miracle will have been born. Right now my wife Kim and I are two weeks away from receiving the gift of a baby boy. We know what it is because we were able to tell during the ultrasound test. That is not all we have grown to know from those moments spent catching a glimpse of a child God sees everyday.

Like many first-time parents we stared at the screen looking for signs of health and life. Our first glimpse of anything recognizable was the top of the baby's head and we only know that because the technician told us. It all looked like shades of gray to me, until suddenly out of the darkness in the upper right corner of the screen came the wave of a tiny little hand. One, two, three, four fingers and a thumb, dear God, it looks sort of like a baby in there! Wrapped safely within an armor of its own grows a child being equipped and prepared for life on the outside.

From this experience I am convinced of two things. One is that the same God who has our son's undivided attention within Kim's womb, will feel a bittersweetness the day our child is born. See, today there is nothing to distract our son from intimacy with God, our Creator. But on the day he is born will come everything else under the sun to infiltrate and distract him from God in his life.

The second thing I am sure of is that the same God longs for the day intimacy with our son will be restored through intimacy with His Son. And with that rebirth will come another kind of armor designed to protect all of God's children from the distractions the enemy sends our way.

> "Finally, be strong in the Lord and in his mighty power. Put on the full armor of God so that you can take your stand against the devil's schemes" (Ephesians 6:10,11).

Some words worth highlighting are:

...be strong

...in his mighty power.

Put on the full armor of God...,

...stand against the devil's schemes.

This section of the book looks at God's armor and leads us to find very practical ways to wear it. It will be a challenge for you to educate students to grasp the value of this information. They must come to know that the armor of God provides much-needed protection for believers as they travel through this earthly life.

As you slip into the armor along with your kids, thank you for caring enough about them to equip them for victory.

DRESSING FOR SUCCESS: THE BELT OF TRUTH; THE BREASTPLATE OF RIGHTEOUSNESS

KEY VERSES

"I pray that out of his glorious riches he may strengthen you with power through his Spirit in your inner being, so that Christ may dwell in your hearts through faith." Ephesians 3:16,17

BIBLICAL BASIS

Proverbs 4:25,26;
Matthew 5:14;
John 8:12,31,32,44; 14:6;
Romans 8:1,10,15,16;
2 Corinthians 10:4,5;
Ephesians 3:16,17,20; 6:10-14;
Philippians 4:13;
2 Timothy 1:6;
1 John 1:5-7; 2:5,6;
Revelation 12:10

THE BIG IDEA

We can stand in victory against the enemy because of the belt of truth and breastplate of righteousness provided for us by God.

AIMS OF THIS SESSION

During this session you will guide students to:

• Examine the belt of truth and the breastplate of righteousness;
• Discover the purpose of truth and righteousness in the believer's life;
• Implement a power-to-grow-on plan.

WARM UP

HOW BRIGHT IS YOUR LIGHT?—

Students discuss their relationship with the light-giving Christ.

TEAM EFFORT— JUNIOR HIGH/ MIDDLE SCHOOL

FIND THE LIE—

Students try to find out which statements about each other are the lies.

TEAM EFFORT— HIGH SCHOOL

TELL THE TRUTH—

Two role-play situations to challenge students to make godly decisions.

IN THE WORD

DRESSING FOR SUCCESS—

A Bible study on truth and righteousness.

THINGS TO THINK ABOUT (OPTIONAL)

Questions to get students thinking and talking about being God's light in the world.

PARENT PAGE

A tool to get the session into the home and allow parents and young people to discuss their brightness level.

DRESSING FOR
SUCCESS:
THE BELT OF
TRUTH; THE
BREASTPLATE OF
RIGHTEOUSNESS

LEADER'S DEVOTIONAL

"Let your eyes look straight ahead, fix your gaze directly before you. Make level paths for your feet and take only ways that are firm" (Proverbs 4:25,26).

I don't know about you, but the vast majority of teenagers I've worked with love amusement parks. Magic Mountain, a wild Southern California amusement park known for such intense rides known as the Viper, Colossus, Batman and the world's first 360 degree loop, the Revolution, is only a couple of hours from our home. One summer, we loaded up the vans and our high school ministry headed out for a day of death-defying, stomach-dropping, head-spinning, throat-clutching, white-knuckler rides. After standing in long, slow lines at the most popular rides, my body was suddenly thrown into a volatile series of torquing twists, spins and drops equal to that of a NASA astronaut training program. I quickly learned to appreciate the mysterious, powerful forces of speed, gravity, thrust and motion.

Though the forces associated with roller coasters are largely invisible when you're zipping down a hundred-foot drop and heading into two successive loops followed by a few corkscrew turns, you're plenty glad to be strapped in by a secure seatbelt. Spend any time at an amusement park and no one will have to convince you of the physical manifestation of unseen forces. What is true of the physical world is equally true of the spiritual world. You need to be strapped in tight!

This chapter will strengthen you and the students in your ministry by teaching you how to strap on the belt of truth and the breastplate of righteousness. As Ephesians 6 tells us, the spiritual forces we fight against are invisible, unseen and deceptively wicked. We are to be strong in the Lord and His mighty power. Our strength is dependent on His strength; we are to yield our will and our power to Him.

Perhaps you've been feeling discouraged lately, feeling trapped on a giant roller coaster of negative situations, uncontrollable circumstances, and up-and-down emotions. Have you perhaps forgotten that you're in a spiritual battle zone, that there are invisible forces out to crush you like a chest-compressing 3-G turn? Prayer is an essential element to strapping on the belt of truth and the breastplate of righteousness. God is ready to meet you in prayer and give you His strength to fight His battles. Be strong in His power and rest in His grace. Though you may feel like you're on an unending roller coaster fighting powerful, unseen forces, Jesus is sitting in the seat right next to you. (Written by Joey O'Connor.)

**"When Jesus comes in, the shadows depart."
—author unknown**

DRESSING FOR SUCCESS: THE BELT OF TRUTH; THE BREASTPLATE OF RIGHTEOUSNESS

KEY VERSES

"I pray that out of his glorious riches he may strengthen you with power through his Spirit in your inner being, so that Christ may dwell in your hearts through faith." Ephesians 3:16,17

BIBLICAL BASIS

Proverbs 4:25,26; Matthew 5:14; John 8:12,31,32,44; 14:6; Romans 8:1,10,15,16; 2 Corinthians 10:4,5; Ephesians 3:16,17,20; 6:10-14; Philippians 4:13; 2 Timothy 1:6; 1 John 1:5-7; 2:5,6; Revelation 12:10

THE BIG IDEA

We can stand in victory against the enemy because of the belt of truth and breastplate of righteousness provided for us by God.

WARM UP (5-10 MINUTES)

HOW BRIGHT IS YOUR LIGHT?

• Divide students into groups of three or four.
• Give each group a copy of "How Bright Is Your Light?" on page 109 and a pen or pencil.
• After giving them a moment to write their answers, have students share in their groups their answers to the following:

Complete the sentence that best describes your relationship with Jesus.
My relationship with Christ is like a neon light because...

My relationship with Christ is like a 100-watt light bulb because...

My relationship with Christ is like a candle because...

Tear along perforation. Fold and place this Bible Tuck-In™ in your Bible for session use.

4. How much darkness is in God according to 1 John 1:5-7?

5. According to John 8:12, what do people that follow Jesus have?

A FINAL QUIZ

_____ + a Believer = Righteousness

What do you think Jesus meant when He said, "For this sums up the Law and the Prophets"?

SO WHAT?

It Glows in the Dark!
First John 1:6,7 explains in detail how to power up your belt of truth.
1. What does it mean to "walk in the light"?

What are three ways you can walk in the light daily?

2. According to 1 John 2:3-6, how do we know we are "in" Jesus?

What is one way you need to be more obedient to God's Word?

THINGS TO THINK ABOUT (OPTIONAL)

• Use the questions on page 112 after or as part of "In the Word."
1. How do people usually recognize a Christian?

2. In Matthew 5:14 Jesus calls believers "the light of the world." What are two ways another Christian has been a light for you?

3. What are two ways you can be God's light for someone today?

PARENT PAGE

• Distribute page to parents.

TEAM EFFORT—JUNIOR HIGH/MIDDLE SCHOOL (15-20 Minutes)

FIND THE LIE

- Give each student a piece of paper and a pen or pencil.
- Have students write three true statements and one false statement about themselves. The false statement needs to be something that could be believable. In groups of three or four, have students read their four statements. The others try to guess which statement is false. Have small prizes for the students that stump the others in their groups.

TEAM EFFORT—HIGH SCHOOL (25-30 Minutes)

TELL THE TRUTH

- Select three guys and three girls to perform the following role-play situations. Give each performer a copy of "Tell the Truth" on page 109.
- Read the descriptions and assign the parts.
- Have the students act out the scenes and then have the group members add anything they might have said or done differently.
- Optional: Give the six students the role-play situations before class begins to give them more time to prepare.

SITUATION ONE (THREE GUYS NEEDED):

Jack is not a Christian but is concerned about doing the right thing. He has been dating his girlfriend for six months and has strong feelings for her. This Saturday she has invited him over to her house for their six-month anniversary dinner. Though Jack's girlfriend has not come right out and said she wants to sleep with him, she has dropped some big hints. Jack needs some advice, so he goes to his two best friends—Tom and Mitch. Tom has been a strong Christian for six years and actually broke up with a girlfriend over the same issue. Mitch isn't a Christian and he's not a bad guy, but does tend to take the worldly approach to decision making. Jack approaches Tom and Mitch for some advice. Ready, Action!

SITUATION TWO (THREE GIRLS NEEDED):

During lunch Jamie walks in on a conversation between two of her friends about abortion. It isn't clear to Jamie that one of the girls is pregnant, but the tension is pretty high. Both Sandy and Lori have seen Jamie walk up, so Jamie can't just leave. Jamie has strong feelings about abortion because her mom had aborted her first baby and hasn't forgiven herself for it. Jamie has seen and heard the pain in her mom's voice on each anniversary of the abortion. Neither Sandy nor Lori know this about Jamie's mom. They turn to Jamie asking her to help them settle their disagreement. First Sandy and Lori share their sides of the issue, then Jamie responds. Ready, Action!

IN THE WORD (25-30 Minutes)

DRESSING FOR SUCCESS

- Divide students into groups of three or four.
- Give each student a copy of "In the Word" on pages 110-111 and pen or pencil, or display a copy using an overhead projector.

- Fold -

- Have students complete the study.
- Option: Divide students into two groups and have one group answer the questions for the section on "The Belt of Truth" and the other group answer the questions on "The Breastplate of Righteousness." Allow time at the end of this section for the two groups to summarize what they learned.

THE BELT OF TRUTH

1. Read Ephesians 6:10,11. Where are believers to find their strength?

What does a believer need to do to receive strength?

2. According to verses 11-13, what is the result of putting on the full armor of God?

3. Paul tells believers to "stand firm then, with the belt of truth buckled around your waist, with the breastplate of righteousness in place" (v. 14). That is some belt and breastplate combo! What do the verses below say about truth and its power?
John 8:31,32

John 14:6

2 Corinthians 10:4,5

Ephesians 3:20

Philippians 4:13

THE BREASTPLATE OF RIGHTEOUSNESS

1. What is righteousness according to Romans 8:1,10,15,16?

2. The breastplate of righteousness which sets us apart as God's child is received when a person puts on the truth of God. Read John 8:44 and Revelation 12:10. Why is the breastplate of righteousness so important to a believer when faced with the enemy's tricks?

3. Paul wasn't kidding when he said in Ephesians 6:10 "be strong in the Lord and in his mighty power." There is power in the truth! John paints a word picture about this powerful truth by introducing a visual comparison of truth in 1 John 1:5-7. What visual does John paint?

DRESSING FOR
SUCCESS:
THE BELT OF
TRUTH; THE
BREASTPLATE OF
RIGHTEOUSNESS

 ARM UP

How Bright Is Your Light?

Complete the sentence that best describes your relationship with Jesus.

My relationship with Christ is like a neon light because...

....

....

My relationship with Christ is like a 100-watt light bulb because...

....

....

My relationship with Christ is like a candle because...

....

....

 EAM EFFORT

Tell the Truth

Situation One (three guys needed):

Jack is not a Christian but is concerned about doing the right thing. He has been dating his girlfriend for six months and has strong feelings for her. This Saturday she has invited him over to her house for their six-month anniversary dinner. Though Jack's girlfriend has not come right out and said she wants to sleep with him, she has dropped some big hints. Jack needs some advice, so he goes to his two best friends—Tom and Mitch. Tom has been a strong Christian for six years and actually broke up with a girlfriend over the same issue. Mitch isn't a Christian and he's not a bad guy, but does tend to take the worldly approach to decision making. Jack approaches Tom and Mitch for some advice. Ready. Action!

Situation Two (three girls needed):

During lunch Jamie walks in on a conversation between two of her friends about abortion. It isn't clear to Jamie that one of the girls is pregnant, but the tension is pretty high. Both Sandy and Lori have seen Jamie walk up, so Jamie can't just leave. Jamie has strong feelings about abortion because her mom had aborted her first baby and hasn't forgiven herself for it. Jamie has seen and heard the pain in her mom's voice on each anniversary of the abortion. Neither Sandy nor Lori know this about Jamie's mom. They turn to Jamie asking her to help them settle their disagreement. First Sandy and Lori share their sides of the issue, then Jamie responds. Ready. Action!

⬤N THE WORD

DRESSING FOR SUCCESS

The Belt of Truth

1. Read Ephesians 6:10,11. Where are believers to find their strength?

What does a believer need to do to receive strength?

2. According to verses 11-13, what is the result of putting on the full armor of God?

3. Paul tells believers to "stand firm then, with the belt of truth buckled around your waist, with the breastplate of righteousness in place" (v. 14). That is some belt and breastplate combo! What do the verses below say about truth and its power?

John 8:31,32

John 14:6

2 Corinthians 10:4,5

Ephesians 3:20

Philippians 4:13

The Breastplate of Righteousness

1. What is righteousness according to Romans 8:1,10,15,16?

2. The breastplate of righteousness, which sets us apart as God's child, is received when a person puts on His truth. Read John 8:44 and Revelation 12:10. Why is the belt of truth and breastplate of righteousness so important to a believer when faced with the enemy's tricks?

IN THE WORD

3. Paul wasn't kidding when he said in Ephesians 6:10 "be strong in the Lord and in his mighty power." There is power in the truth! John paints a word picture about this powerful truth by introducing a visual comparison of truth in 1 John 1:5-7. What visual does John paint?

....

....

4. How much darkness is in God according to 1 John 1:5-7?

....

....

5. According to John 8:12, what do people that follow Jesus have?

....

....

A Final Quiz

.... + a Believer = Righteousness

SO WHAT?

It Glows in the Dark!
First John 1:6,7 explains in detail how to power up your belt of truth.

1. What does it mean to "walk in the light"?

....

....

What are three ways you can walk in the light daily?

....

....

2. According to 1 John 2:3-6, how do we know we are "in" Jesus?

....

....

What is one way you need to be more obedient to God's Word?

....

....

DRESSING FOR
SUCCESS:
THE BELT OF
TRUTH; THE
BREASTPLATE OF
RIGHTEOUSNESS

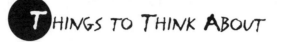

THINGS TO THINK ABOUT

1. How do people usually recognize a Christian?

   ....
   ....
   ....

2. In Matthew 5:14 Jesus calls believers "the light of the world." What are two ways another Christian has been a light for you?

   ....
   ....
   ....

3. What are two ways you can be God's light for someone today?

   ....
   ....
   ....

PARENT PAGE

LIGHT MY FIRE, LORD

Get a candle, light it and put it where you can see it. By candlelight, share with each other the answers to these questions:

1. What is one great memory you have when you think of using a candle?

2. How does a candle work?

3. There are four stages to a candle's light:
   1. Pre-lit   2. Burning   3. Blown Out   4. Burned Out

   Which stage best describes your relationship with God at present?

4. In Ephesians 6:14, Paul tells us how to stand firm. How are we to stand firm?

5. In what way does John compare truth to light in 1 John 1:6,7?

6. Out of concern for Timothy, what does Paul challenge him to do with his flame in 2 Timothy 1:6?

7. There is no doubt that truth wins the battles against the enemy's influence in our lives. Share with one another what you can do to help each other follow Paul's encouragement to Timothy to fan the flame.

Session 9 "Dressing for Success: The Belt of Truth; the Breastplate of Righteousness"

Date ....

KNOWING WHAT YOU BELIEVE, BELIEVING WHAT YOU KNOW: THE GOSPEL OF PEACE; THE SHIELD OF FAITH

KEY VERSE

"Stand firm then…with your feet fitted with the readiness that comes from the gospel of peace. In addition to all this, take up the shield of faith, with which you can extinguish all the flaming arrows of the evil one."
Ephesians 6:14-16

BIBLICAL BASIS

John 1:14; 3:17; 10:10;
Acts 2:22-24;
Romans 6:1-11; 8:1-4; 10:17;
2 Corinthians 5:7,17-19;
Ephesians 4:1,2; 5:1,2,8-10; 6:13-16;
Philippians 1:27,28;
Colossians 3:17;
1 Thessalonians 5:10;
1 Timothy 4:12; 6:11-14;
Hebrews 9:15;
James 1:6;
1 Peter 3:15,18;
1 John 4:10

THE BIG IDEA

The depth of our beliefs can make us confident in what we know. That confidence in God leads to victory.

AIMS OF THIS SESSION

During this session you will guide students to:
• Examine the gospel of peace and the shield of faith;
• Discover the effects of the gospel of peace on a believer's life;
• Implement a shield-of-faith protection plan.

WARM UP

A ROLLER COASTER DREAM—

Students design their dream roller coaster and relate it to real life.

TEAM EFFORT— JUNIOR HIGH/ MIDDLE SCHOOL

PING PONG SLALOM—

A game to illustrate the truth of James 1:6.

TEAM EFFORT— HIGH SCHOOL

BOTTOM BEACH BALL VOLLEY—

A game to demonstrate defending oneself from Satan's attacks.

IN THE WORD

KNOW WHAT YOU BELIEVE, FIGHT FOR WHAT YOU KNOW—

A Bible study on the gospel of peace and the shield of faith.

THINGS TO THINK ABOUT (OPTIONAL)

Questions to get students thinking and talking about making God-centered decisions.

PARENT PAGE

A tool to get the session into the home and allow parents and young people to discuss how their shield of faith in Christ has been evident in their lives.

KNOWING WHAT
YOU BELIEVE,
BELIEVING WHAT
YOU KNOW:
THE GOSPEL OF
PEACE; THE SHIELD
OF FAITH

LEADER'S DEVOTIONAL

"The Word became flesh and made his dwelling among us. We have seen his glory, the glory of the One and Only, who came from the Father, full of grace and truth" (John 1:14).

Have you ever spoken with a student who was hung-up on trying to figure out what they believe? Ever faced a teenage interrogator in one of those, "Yeah, but-what-about-this-well-if-not-that-then-how-come..."conversations? Every youth ministry is filled with a number of inquisitive students who are asking, seeking, postulating, theorizing and attempting to honestly dig into the mind of the Almighty. I think God purposely puts at least one student like this in every youth group just to keep the adult leaders on their toes. Who knows? Perhaps in ten to twenty years, these kids will be leading theologians.

I don't have to tell you the importance of knowing what you believe. What we believe and how we act on what we believe is critical to our faith development. What we believe will also greatly influence our perspective on spiritual warfare. Knowing God's Word and the truth of historical Christianity are powerful assets in warding off Satan's attacks on our hearts and minds. All that said, knowing what you believe isn't as significant as knowing Who you believe in. God did not send a "what" to die on a cross for our sins. He sent a "Who," a Person, his only Son, Jesus Christ. Christianity is a Who, not a what.

With the constant help of the Holy Spirit, we can meet Jesus every day by discovering who He is in His word. Applying what we learn about Who we believe in, we can grow in His grace and wisdom. This is just one of many ways to develop the faith of young believers. Your students' perplexing questions, ranging from the evolution of dinosaur brains to the existence of a pet heaven, to whether or not Jesus hung out at 7-11 as a teenager are vital to their faith and intellectual developments. If it's important to them, then it should be important to you. But one thing you'll want to be sure to do is to steer them back into the direction of a Savior with dusty sandals, sweat on His brow, hands that healed and eyes filled with tears—God in human flesh.

Grasping, knowing and experiencing the living Jesus is much more satisfying and intimate than knowing archeological facts, temple weight figures and Bible maps. Only by knowing Jesus, this man from Nazareth, will you, your students and I be able to experience peace and victory in the spiritual battles we fight each day. Jesus is not what we believe in, but Who we believe in. (Written by Joey O'Connor.)

"We need the power that comes from being certain that God is there, so sure of His love that we can work on in confidence at the task before us."
—Gloria Gaither

SESSION TEN

BIBLE TUCK-IN™

KNOWING WHAT YOU BELIEVE, BELIEVING WHAT YOU KNOW: THE GOSPEL OF PEACE; THE SHIELD OF FAITH

KEY VERSES

"Stand firm then...with your feet fitted with the readiness that comes from the gospel of peace. In addition to all this, take up the shield of faith, with which you can extinguish all the flaming arrows of the evil one." Ephesians 6:14-16

BIBLICAL BASIS

John 1:14; 3:17; 10:10; Acts 2:22-24; Romans 6:1-11; 8:1-4; 10:17; 2 Corinthians 5:7,17-19; Ephesians 4:1,2; 5:1,2,8-10; 6:13-16; Philippians 1:27,28; Colossians 3:17; 1 Thessalonians 5:10; 1 Timothy 4:12; 5:12; 6:11-14; Hebrews 9:15; James 1:6; 1 Peter 3:15,18; 1 John 4:10

THE BIG IDEA

The depth of our beliefs can make us confident in what we know. That confidence leads to victory.

WARM UP (5-10 MINUTES)

A ROLLER COASTER DREAM

• Divide students into groups of three or four.
• Give each group a large piece of posterboard or butcher paper and several felt-tip pens or crayons.
• Tell them to design their dream roller coaster.
• Give the groups some time to share their designs.
• Discuss the following question:
  Momma says "life is a lot like a roller coaster." In what ways is this statement true?

---- Fold ----

117

Your Group's Statement of Faith

SO WHAT?

1. What does knowing what you believe do for your faith in Christ?

2. What does Romans 10:17 say is the result of studying God's word?

3. According to Ephesians 6:16, why do we need a shield of faith?

4. What are some of the flaming arrows the enemy has used to wound you so that it is hard to continue standing firm behind your shield of faith?

5. What can you do to strengthen your shield of faith in order to defend yourself?

THINGS TO THINK ABOUT (OPTIONAL)

• Use the questions on page 121 after or as part of "In the Word."
1. Why did Christ come to earth?

2. While He was on earth, what was the most significant thing that He did?

3. In what way is your life different because of His sacrifice?

PARENT PAGE

• Distribute page to parents.

TEAM EFFORT—JUNIOR HIGH/ MIDDLE SCHOOL (15-20 MINUTES)

PING PONG SLALOM

- Divide students into teams of five or six.
- Have students line up in teams one behind the other.
- Set the same number of paper cups upside down on the floor about every three to four feet in a line in front of each team.
- Give each team a ping pong ball.
- Instruct students that when you say go, the first person on each team must get down on hands and knees and blow the ping pong ball back and forth around the cups up and back to the next person in line. When the first person touches the foot of the next person in line, that person gets down on hands and knees and does the same thing. Play continues until everyone in line has had a turn.
- The first team that finishes the slalom course is the winner.
- Discuss the following questions:
1. What made this game an easy game to play?
2. What made it difficult?
3. James 1:6 says "he who doubts is like a wave...blown and tossed by the wind." How does this game illustrate the truth in that verse?
4. How would the game change if you were trying to blow a rock around the course? How does that relate to James 1:6?

TEAM EFFORT—HIGH SCHOOL (15-20 MINUTES)

BOTTOM BEACH BALL VOLLEY

- Place two chairs about 12 to 15 feet apart across the middle of the room. Tie a string, rope or volleyball net to the chairs.
- Divide students into two equal teams.
- Have each team sit on the floor facing the "net."
- The students will hit a beach ball back and forth across the "net" trying to keep it off the floor while keeping their bottoms on the floor. Any team that has a member get up off the floor to hit the ball loses possession of the ball and it is counted as a score for the other team if the other team "served" the ball. The game is scored just like volleyball.
- Discuss the following questions:
1. The winning team had to keep the ball from landing on the floor on their side of the net. How did the winning team defend its space?
2. How do Christians defend themselves from the enemy's attacks?

IN THE WORD (25-30 MINUTES)

KNOW WHAT YOU BELIEVE, FIGHT FOR WHAT YOU KNOW

- Divide students into groups of three or four.
- Give each student a copy of "In the Word" on pages 119-121 and a pen or pencil, or display a copy using an overhead projector.

- Have students complete the Bible study.
- Leave time for the groups to share their "statements of faith."

Your statement of faith needs to include the answers to the following questions.

1. **What was your Captain fighting for?**

   John 3:17 ....

   John 10:10 ....

   1 John 4:10 ....

2. **What did He gain from dying for the cause?**

   1 Thessalonians 5:10 ....

   Hebrews 9:15 ....

   1 Peter 3:18 ....

3. **What happened that secured the victory?**

   Acts 2:22-24 ....

   Romans 6:1-11 ....

4. **How did the victory affect His followers?**

   Romans 6:1-8 ....

   Romans 8:1-4 ....

   2 Corinthians 5:17-19 ....

5. **How are His followers to live as a result of what He has done for them?**

   Ephesians 4:1,2 ....

   Ephesians 5:1,2,8-10 ....

   Colossians 3:17 ....

6. **What does it mean to stand for the cause?**

   Philippians 1:27,28 ....

   1 Timothy 6:11-14 ....

   1 Peter 3:15 ....

7. **How do His followers fight for the cause?**

   2 Corinthians 5:7 ....

   1 Timothy 4:12 ....

   1 Timothy 6:12 ....

KNOWING WHAT
YOU BELIEVE,
BELIEVING WHAT
YOU KNOW:
THE GOSPEL OF
PEACE; THE SHIELD
OF FAITH

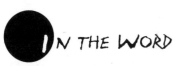 N THE WORD

KNOW WHAT YOU BELIEVE, FIGHT FOR WHAT YOU KNOW

"Therefore put on the full armor of God, so that when the day of evil comes, you may be able to stand your ground, and after you have done everything, to stand" (Ephesians 6:13) Your group is a small yet essential part of a larger group of revolutionaries fighting for what is rightfully yours. Your Captain won the battle for your freedom, but to do so He willingly sacrificed His life. He leaves your team with a very important task. It is your job to use the weapons He left behind to create a statement of faith for others who come behind you to follow. The first weapon left for you is our guidebook—the Bible—that gives you all the information you'll need to write your statement. It is essential that you know what you believe. The second weapon is the shield of faith for every member of the army. It's with this shield of faith that you'll be able to protect yourselves from the attack of the enemy. The references below contain the facts you'll use to write a statement of faith (what you believe). Be sure to study them carefully.

Your statement of faith needs to include the answers to the following questions.

1. What was your Captain fighting for?

John 3:17 ....

John 10:10 ....

1 John 4:10 ....

....

2. What did He gain from dying for the cause?

1 Thessalonians 5:10 ....

Hebrews 9:15 ....

1 Peter 3:18 ....

....

3. What happened that secured the victory?

Acts 2:22-24 ....

Romans 6:1-11 ....

....

KNOWING WHAT
YOU BELIEVE,
BELIEVING WHAT
YOU KNOW:
THE GOSPEL OF
PEACE; THE SHIELD
OF FAITH

IN THE WORD

4. How did the victory affect His followers?

Romans 6:1-8 ....

....

Romans 8:1-4 ....

....

2 Corinthians 5:17-19 ....

....

5. How are His followers to live as a result of what He has done for them?

Ephesians 4:1,2 ....

....

Ephesians 5:1,2, 8-10 ....

....

Colossians 3:17 ....

....

6. What does it mean to stand for the cause?

Philippians 1:27,28 ....

....

1 Timothy 6:11-14 ....

....

1 Peter 3:15 ....

....

7. How do His followers fight for the cause?

2 Corinthians 5:7 ....

....

1 Timothy 4:12 ....

....

1 Timothy 6:12 ....

....

Your Group's Statement of Faith

....

....

IN THE WORD

SO WHAT?

1. What does knowing what you believe do for your faith in Christ?

2. What does Romans 10:17 say is the result of studying God's word?

3. According to Ephesians 6:16, why do we need a shield of faith?

4. What are some of the flaming arrows the enemy has used to wound you so that it is hard to continue standing firm behind your shield of faith?

5. What can you do to strengthen your shield of faith in order to defend yourself?

THINGS TO THINK ABOUT

1. Why did Christ come to earth?

2. While He was on earth, what was the most significant thing that He did?

3. In what way is your life different because of it?

KNOWING WHAT
YOU BELIEVE,
BELIEVING WHAT
YOU KNOW:
THE GOSPEL OF
PEACE; THE SHIELD
OF FAITH

PARENT PAGE

BELIEVE IT AND CHANGE

1. Read Romans 5:6-11 and check the following words that best describe how you feel about what God has done for us through Christ.
   - ❑ Thankful
   - ❑ Grateful
   - ❑ Guilty
   - ❑ Blessed
   - ❑ Fortunate
   - ❑ Peaceful
   - ❑ Confident
   - ❑ Appreciative
   - ❑ Loving
   - ❑ Committed
   - ❑ Forgiven

2. What do you appreciate most about what Christ did for us? Why?

   ....

   ....

3. How has your faith in Christ grown as you have learned more about Him?

   ....

   ....

4. According to Ephesians 6:13,15,16, what does our strong faith in the gospel of Christ do for us in battle against the enemy?

   ....

   ....

5. Parent: Give at least two examples of experiences where your shield of faith saved you from an attack of the enemy.

   ....

   ....

6. Student: Give at least two examples of experiences where your shield of faith saved you from an attack of the enemy.

   ....

   ....

Session 10 "Knowing What You Believe,
Believing What You Know: The Gospel of Peace;
the Shield of Faith" Date ....

COVER YOUR HEAD AND SWING YOUR SWORD: THE HELMET OF SALVATION; THE SWORD OF THE SPIRIT

Key Verses

"Consider it pure joy, my brothers, whenever you face trials of many kinds." James 1:2

Biblical Basis

Nehemiah 8:10;
Psalm 19:7;
Proverbs 3:5,6;
Luke 10:19,20;
Romans 5:3-5; 15:13;
2 Corinthians 3:4,5; 10:4,5;
Ephesians 6:17;
Philippians 4:13;
1 Thessalonians 5:8;
2 Timothy 2:15;
Hebrews 4:12,13; 10:23;
James 1:2

The Big Idea

Our attitude choices can set the course for the outcome of the battle. The victory comes when we choose an attitude of trust in God.

Aims of This Session

During this session you will guide students to:
- Examine the helmet of salvation and the sword of the Spirit;
- Discover the power for spiritual victory that comes in choosing an attitude of trust in God;
- Implement the choice to have a positive attitude.

Warm Up

I Like Life Because...—
Students list the reasons they like life.

Team Effort—Junior High/Middle School

"I Can" Banner—
Students share thoughts on how they can improve the world.

Team Effort—High School

Truth or Consequence—
A game that illustrates making wise choices.

In the Word

Hattitude Check—
A Bible study on the helmet of salvation and the sword of the Spirit.

Things to Think About (OPTIONAL)

Questions to get students thinking and talking about how they can choose to put on a good attitude.

Parent Page

A tool to get the session into the home and allow parents and young people to discuss how they can choose to trust God.

COVER YOUR HEAD
AND SWING YOUR
SWORD:
THE HELMET OF
SALVATION;
THE SWORD OF
THE SPIRIT

LEADER'S DEVOTIONAL

"The law of the Lord is perfect, reviving the soul. The statutes of the Lord are trustworthy, making wise the simple" (Psalm 19:7).

One of my all-time favorite movies is "The Mission," starring Robert DeNiro and Jeremy Irons. Set during the Portuguese colonial period in South America, this outstanding film depicts the Christian conversion of a Portuguese slave trader. (This is a "must-see" movie!) In one of the most gripping scenes, Robert DeNiro is seen dragging a net full of burdensome weapons and armor up huge cliffs and dangerous waterfalls. Exhausted and covered in mud, he falls at the feet of the jungle Indians he formerly chased, captured and sold off into slavery. Grabbing a knife, one of the Indians dashes to a broken and bruised DeNiro and appears to be ready to quickly execute his enemy. Surprisingly, the Indian grabs the rope attaching DeNiro's burden to his chest and cuts him free. Overwhelmed with the grace of forgiveness, the former slave trader bursts into tears as the priests and Indians laugh and rejoice in this remarkable act of freedom. DeNiro's weapons are thrown off the cliff and he enters a whole new realm of freedom in Christ. However, he also enters into a new spiritual arena of battle when the Portuguese government begins to shut down the church's missions. DeNiro is now a soldier in God's army.

Exchanging swords of steel for the sword of the Spirit, history is filled with amazing conversions. A steel sword can pierce the heart, yet only the sword of the Spirit can break it. Warriors have fought bloody battles throughout history protected by all sorts of armor. Because we are protected by the helmet of salvation, we can learn to face spiritual battles with freedom, confidence and hope in Christ.

One of the tricks—call it a flat-out-rotten-smelling lie—Satan will use to discourage you as a youth worker is to keep reminding you about past sins, mistakes and character flaws. Just like that filthy net of old weapons and battle armor Robert DeNiro dragged beind him, Satan uses guilt and shame to drag you down by reminding you of sins that have already been forgiven. In Christ, you have been freed of your former life, or as Paul calls it, the "old man." That good-for-nothing baggage has been cut off and rolled straight off a cliff. You are now free to love and enjoy an intimate relationship with God. The Holy Spirit gives you the secure hope of your salvation and the sword of the Spirit enables you to plant the seeds of God's word into young lives. Formerly enemies of God, we are now His children with a purpose-filled mission. Rent "The Mission"… it's worth the two bucks. Live God's mission; it's worth eternity. (Written by Joey O'Connor.)

**"The helmet of salvation reminds us that we belong to Jesus and that we are assured of final victory in battle."
—C. Peter Wagner**

Tear along perforation. Fold and place this Bible *Tuck-In*™ 'm your bible for session use.

COVER YOUR HEAD AND SWING YOUR SWORD: THE HELMET OF SALVATION; THE SWORD OF THE SPIRIT

KEY VERSE

"Consider it pure joy, my brothers, whenever you face trials of many kinds." James 1:2

BIBLICAL BASIS

Nehemiah 8:10; Psalm 19:7; Proverbs 3:5,6; Luke 10:19,20; Romans 5:3-5; 15:13; 2 Corinthians 3:4,5; 10:4,5; Ephesians 6:17; Philippians 4:13; 1 Thessalonians 5:8; 2 Timothy 2:15; Hebrews 4:12,13; 10:23; James 1:2

THE BIG IDEA

Our attitude choices can set the course for the outcome of the battle. The victory comes when we choose an attitude of trust in God.

WARM UP (5-10 MINUTES)

I LIKE LIFE BECAUSE...

• Give each student a copy of "I Like Life Because…" on page 127 and a pen or pencil.
• Have them complete the page and then share some of their answers.
List 10 reasons you like life.

1. I like life because...
2. I like life because...
3. I like life because...
4. I like life because...
5. I like life because...
6. I like life because...
7. I like life because...
8. I like life because...
9. I like life because...
10. I like life because...

---- Fold ----

2. Who is the source of power for our I-can attitude? What does that mean to you?

3. What are three battles you are facing in which you are struggling to maintain a winning attitude?

4. What are three things you can do to change your attitude and thus pave the way for victory?

THINGS TO THINK ABOUT (OPTIONAL)

• Use the questions on page 130 after or as part of "In the Word."
1. What do you think causes people to have bad attitudes?

2. Nehemiah 8:10 says "the joy of the Lord is your strength." If this is true then what do you think would be the opposite of joy and how does that opposite attitude affect believers?

3. Having a positive attitude is your choice. What are some attitude changes you know you have to make?

What will you do to change these bad attitudes?

PARENT PAGE

• Distribute page to parents.

TEAM EFFORT—JUNIOR HIGH/MIDDLE SCHOOL (15-20 MINUTES)

"I CAN..." BANNER

- Tape a long piece of butcher paper on a wall and in bold letters write across the top "I can..."
- Have several water-soluble felt-tip pens available for the students to write down as many positive things as they can think of that they can do to make the world a better place in which to live.
- Read through the ideas together and have each student agree to work at one of the actions during the next week.

TEAM EFFORT—HIGH SCHOOL (15-20 MINUTES)

TRUTH OR CONSEQUENCE

- Give each student four 3x5-inch cards and a pen or pencil.
- Ask them to write a different inquisitive-style question on two of the cards. For example: How would you describe a good attitude? What is something that makes you angry?
- On each of the other two cards have them write a simple action. For example: Sing "The Star Spangled Banner" while hopping on one foot. Remind the students that they might pick their own cards so that they don't get too silly with their consequences.
- Collect all of the cards keeping the two different types separate and shuffle them placing the two piles on the floor in the center of the room.
- Have the students form a circle on the floor around the piles of cards.
- The leader will start by flipping a coin. If the coin lands on heads, the first player chooses a card from either the "Truth" pile or the "Consequence" pile. They must either answer the truth question or do the consequence action. If the coin lands on tails, the player has the option of: (a) Choosing a card from either pile and doing what it says, or (b) Asking a question of anyone in the room or asking them to do a consequence.
- Discuss the following questions:
  1. Which do you like better—truth or consequence? Why?
  2. In what ways is life like this game?
  3. How can a change of attitude affect a specific situation?

IN THE WORD (25-30 MINUTES)

HATTITUDE CHECK

- Divide students into groups of three or four.
- Give each student a copy of "In the Word" on pages 128-129 and a pen or pencil, or display a copy using an overhead projector.
- Have students complete the Bible study.

Romans 15:13

1. What does the helmet of salvation do?

---

1 Thessalonians 5:8

Hebrews 10:23

2. The helmet of salvation fills our minds with hope. In a battle against the enemy, what good is hope?

3. Hope can secure our victory. What do these verses say about the power we can have hope in?

Luke 10:19,20

2 Corinthians 3:4,5

CHECK YOUR WEAPON

1. We have been given the most powerful offensive weapon to be used against the enemy. According to Ephesians 6:17, what is the sword of the Spirit?

2. How does Hebrews 4:12,13 describe the sword of the Spirit?

3. What does verse 13 say is hidden from God's sight? How does that affect you?

4. According to 2 Corinthians 10:4,5 what can the weapons with which we fight accomplish?

5. Second Timothy 2:15 says "Do your best to present yourself to God as one approved, a workman who does not need to be ashamed and who correctly handles the word of truth." What does that mean?

6. Like any weapon, the sword of the Spirit, if misused, can do much harm. What are three ways to use the sword for good and three ways to use the sword to do harm?

Good:

Harm:

SO WHAT?

A Good Attitude Is Everything.

1. Paul sets us up for victory in Philippians 4:13 by telling us about choosing an "I-can" attitude. What does he say we can do?

I LIKE LIFE BECAUSE...

List 10 reasons you like life.

1. I like life because... ....

2. I like life because... ....

3. I like life because... ....

4. I like life because... ....

5. I like life because... ....

6. I like life because... ....

7. I like life because... ....

8. I like life because... ....

9. I like life because... ....

10. I like life because... ....

COVER YOUR HEAD
AND SWING YOUR
SWORD:
THE HELMET OF
SALVATION;
THE SWORD OF
THE SPIRIT

PUTTING ON GOD'S ARMOR

◐N THE WORD

HATTITUDE CHECK

1. What does the helmet of salvation do?

Romans 15:13 ....

1 Thessalonians 5:8 ....

Hebrews 10:23 ....

2. The helmet of salvation fills our minds with hope. In a battle against the enemy, what good is hope?

....

....

....

3. Hope can secure our victory. What do these verses say about the power we can have hope in?

Luke 10:19,20 ....

2 Corinthians 3:4,5 ....

Check Your Weapon

1. We have been given the most powerful offensive weapon to be used against the enemy. According to Ephesians 6:17, what is the sword of the Spirit?

....

....

2. How does Hebrews 4:12,13 describe the sword of the Spirit?

....

....

3. What does verse 13 say is hidden from God's sight? How does that affect you?

....

....

....

COVER YOUR HEAD
AND SWING YOUR
SWORD:
THE HELMET OF
SALVATION;
THE SWORD OF
THE SPIRIT

IN THE WORD

4. According to 2 Corinthians 10:4,5 what can the weapons with which we fight accomplish?

....

....

5. Second Timothy 2:15 says "Do your best to present yourself to God as one approved, a workman who does not need to be ashamed and who correctly handles the word of truth." What does that mean?

....

....

6. Like any weapon, the sword of the Spirit, if misused, can do much harm. What are three ways to use the sword for good and three ways to use the sword to do harm?

Good: ....

....

....

Harm: ....

....

....

SO WHAT?

A Good Attitude is Everything

1. Paul sets us up for victory in Philippians 4:13 by telling us about choosing an "I-can" attitude. What does he say we can do?

....

....

2. Who is the source of power for our I-can attitude? What does that mean to you?

....

....

3. What are three battles you are facing in which you are struggling to maintain a winning attitude?

....

....

4. What are three things you can do to change your attitude and thus pave the way for victory?

....

....

COVER YOUR HEAD
AND SWING YOUR
SWORD:
THE HELMET OF
SALVATION;
THE SWORD OF
THE SPIRIT

THINGS TO THINK ABOUT

1. What do you think causes people to have bad attitudes?

....

....

....

2. Nehemiah 8:10 says the "joy of the Lord is your strength." If this is true then what do you think would be the opposite of joy and how does that opposite attitude affect believers?

....

....

....

3. Having a positive attitude is your choice. What are some attitude changes you know you have to make?

....

....

....

What will you do to change these bad attitudes?

....

....

....

COVER YOUR HEAD
AND SWING YOUR
SWORD:
THE HELMET OF
SALVATION;
THE SWORD OF
THE SPIRIT

 PARENT PAGE

CHOOSING TO TRUST

The story is told about a famous family of trapeze performers on the day they began to train the youngest daughter to "fly." The father coached his daughter up to the high trapeze at the top of the training tent. There she stood many feet above the tent floor. Below her was a safety net, but she was not harnessed to any type of safety cable. He allowed her to stand there for a few minutes before he instructed the trapeze to be released.

The daughter turned to her father and said, "Daddy I am afraid, please let me come down."

Her father's loving reply was "Trust me, I know how you feel. Just throw your heart towards the bar and your body will follow."

1. In Proverbs 3:5,6, we have a similar coaxing from our heavenly Father. What does the passage tell us to do?

....

....

2. What does this passage say the result of trusting God will be?

....

....

3. Share with each other one area in your life where you find it hard to choose to trust God.

....

4. Now tell each other why you find it so hard to choose to trust Him.

....

....

5. In Romans 5:3-5, Paul states the result of choosing to rejoice in our struggles. What do we miss out on if we choose to do our own thing?

....

....

6. Share with each other the choice you will make today about your attitude toward your struggles and what you will do differently because of your attitude change.

Pray for each other about the changes in attitude that you want to make and how you can support one another in making these changes.

Session 11 "Cover Your Head and Swing Your Sword:
The Helmet of Salvation; the Sword of the Spirit"
Date ....

CONSTANT CONTACT WITH THE COMMANDER-IN-CHIEF

K EY VERSES

"And pray in the Spirit on all occasions with all kinds of prayers and requests. With this in mind, be alert and always keep on praying for all the saints." Ephesians 6:18

B IBLICAL BASIS

Joshua 1:1-9;
Psalm 5:2,3;
Matthew 14:22-33; 16:13-19;
Ephesians 6:18;
Philippians 4:4-7;
1 Thessalonians 5:21;
James 1:5-7; 4:2,3

T HE BIG IDEA

No battle is won without careful planning and consultation with the Commander-in-Chief. In order to secure victory in the midst of spiritual battles, we must maintain our communication link—prayer—with our Commander.

A IMS OF THIS SESSION

During this session you will guide students to:

• Examine the key components of communication with their Commander;
• Discover why victories are lost due to the lack of communication;
• Implement a prayer communication contract.

W ARM UP

IF I WERE GOD...—
Students list what they would do if they were God.

T EAM EFFORT— JUNIOR HIGH/ MIDDLE SCHOOL

WORD SCULPTURE—
A game to illustrate communication difficulties.

T EAM EFFORT— HIGH SCHOOL

LISTEN AND LEARN—
A game to demonstrate the role of listening in communication.

I N THE WORD

A CONVERSATION WITH THE COMMANDER—
A Bible study on how to communicate with God in prayer.

T HINGS TO THINK ABOUT (OPTIONAL)

Questions to get students thinking and talking about their own prayer habits.

P ARENT PAGE

A tool to get the session into the home and allow parents and young people to discuss prayer.

CONSTANT CONTACT WITH THE COMMANDER-IN-CHIEF

LEADER'S DEVOTIONAL

"Listen to my cry for help, my King and my God, for to you I pray. In the morning, O Lord, you hear my voice; in the morning I lay my requests before you and wait in expectation" (Psalm 5:2,3).

When I played volleyball in college, my team's favorite diversion during water breaks was to shoot baskets with the volleyball. My favorite shot was the heart-stopping, half-court last second at the buzzer toss to the orange metal rim. Swiissh! It was a shot I didn't make too often. Lobbing the volleyball high into the air, my shots usually fell desperately short, went long into the stands or smacked against the acrylic backboard with a reverberating thud. A basketball player I was not, and am still not.

There have been periods in my life when my prayer life has been very similar to those throw 'em up half-court prayer shots. The results? Air balls. Inconsistency. Missed rims. Few points. Frustration.

When we pray, we neither gain nor lose points with God. There's no scoreboard in heaven that reads: God-Infinity, Joey-2. Prayer is our way to know and communicate with God. Too often, I dismiss the importance of prayer until a really big ticket item comes along and I think, "Oh boy, I'd better pray about this one!" So, I toss up a half-court prayer shot, turn around, walk away and usually forget whether or not God answered my prayer. In strictly basketball terms, not too many games are won at half-court. The same is true for prayer and spiritual battle.

We are to pray consistently and constantly. We are to pray believing God will hear and answer our prayers. We pray to know and worship God. Expectantly, we pray to listen to God's voice as He whispers to our soul. We pray to know God. Follow Him. Love Him. Serve Him. Abide in Him. As C.S. Lewis said, "I don't pray to change me. I pray because prayer changes me." Prayer will equip you to fight the tests, temptations and trials you face each day. Prayer will change you and it will change the lives of the students you minister to. Seek God fervently in prayer today. By maintaining constant communication with your Heavenly Father, you'll never have to throw a desperate prayer shot at the buzzer. (Written by Joey O'Connor.)

"I have been driven many times to my knees by the overwhelming conviction that I had nowhere else to go. My own wisdom, and that of all about me, seemed insufficient for the day."
—Abraham Lincoln

CONSTANT CONTACT WITH THE COMMANDER-IN-CHIEF

KEY VERSE

"And pray in the Spirit on all occasions with all kinds of prayers and requests. With this in mind, be alert and always keep on praying for all the saints." Ephesians 6:18

BIBLICAL BASIS

Joshua 1:1-9; Psalm 5:2,3; Matthew 14:22-33; 16:13-19; Ephesians 6:18; Philippians 4:4-7; 1 Thessalonians 5:21; James 1:5-7; 4:2,3

THE BIG IDEA

No battle is won without careful planning and consultation with the Commander-in-Chief. In order to secure victory in the midst of spiritual battles, we must maintain our communication link—prayer—with our Commander.

WARM UP (5-10 MINUTES)

IF I WERE GOD...

• Have students find a partner to work with.
• Give each pair a copy of "If I Were God..." on page 137 and a pen or pencil.
• Have students work together to complete the list.
• If time allows, have students share at least one of their completions.
List 10 things you would do differently if you were God today.

TEAM EFFORT—JUNIOR HIGH/
MIDDLE SCHOOL (15-20 MINUTES)

WORD SCULPTURE

• You will need enough modeling clay or dough for each group to mold the listed objects.
• Beforehand write each of the following words on a separate slip of paper:

volleyball	telephone	baby bottle
poodle	tuba	rake

---

4. Peter takes the belief-or-doubt challenge in Matthew 14:22-33. What happens to Peter that brings him to confidently say "truly you are the Son of God" in Matthew 14:33?

COMPONENT THREE: PRAY SPECIFICALLY.

1. In Matthew 14:29, Jesus asks Peter to step out of the boat and walk on the water. In verse 28, Peter demonstrates the third component of prayer—to pray specifically for what you need. Even though this verse is not stated in the form of a question, what was Peter specifically asking Jesus to reveal to him?

2. What is Jesus' immediate response?

3. What does James 4:2 say is the reason we don't have answers to our prayers?

COMPONENT FOUR: PRAY EXPECTING TO HEAR GOD'S VOICE.

1. After asking God specifically for something, most Christians get up from praying and walk out thinking: It is all over. I've done my part. What does Matthew 16:17 say that points to Component Four of victorious prayer? In other words how did Peter know the answer to Jesus' question (v. 17)?

2. Peter listened for Christ's response. So many Christians leave their prayer time before the Lord has a chance to respond to their questions. What are the five specific statements that Jesus makes in His response to Peter in Matthew 16:17-19?
   a. The blessing:
   b. A confirmation that Peter had heard God correctly:
   c. A name change:
   d. A life purpose:
   e. The equipment to live out that purpose:

So WHAT?

A Prayer Plan

The best way to pray to win is to practice. Here is a simple structure you can use to prepare yourself for a winning conversation with God. The structure is based on Philippians 4:4-7. It can be done verbally, silently or in a prayer journal. It is much easier to remember the thoughts and verses you may hear while listening when you write them down in a journal or on a note pad. The greatest battles are won in prayer. Take the time to practice step-by-step as a group using the structure below.

THINGS TO THINK ABOUT (OPTIONAL)

• Use the questions on page 142 after or as part of "In the Word."
1. What are two ways you have seen prayer work in your life or in the life of someone you know?

2. What is one thing that you would ask God to do for you right now if He were standing in the room?

3. What keeps you from asking Him everyday in prayer to meet your needs and/or for His help?

PARENT PAGE

• Distribute page to parents.

scissors
elephant
Volkswagen
football helmet
nose

- Divide students into groups of four to six members each and have them sit around a table or in a circle on the floor with a piece of cardboard on which to "sculpt" the words.
- Tell students that they will be given a word to "sculpt" out of modeling clay or dough. The "sculptors" may not say anything to their team members except yes or no in answer to their guesses.
- Give each group a portion of the modeling clay or dough.
- Each group needs to choose who will be the first "sculptor". That person will gather around the cue person at the front of the room. The cue person will show them the first word. When the leader says go, the sculptors run back to their own group and begin to create the object out of the clay or dough until someone from the team guesses the word correctly. The first team to identify the word gets a point.

The play continues with the next sculptors getting another word from the cue person. The game is completed when you either run out of words or time.
- Discuss the following questions:
  1. Was this a difficult game? Why or why not?
  2. Communicating clearly is tough. What made communication difficult in this game?

𝕋EAM EFFORT—HIGH SCHOOL (15-20 MINUTES)

LISTEN AND LEARN
- Divide students into pairs.
- Give each student a blank piece of paper and a pen or pencil and have them sit back-to-back on the floor with one partner facing the front of the room.
- The lead students that are facing the front of the room will draw a simple picture and as they draw they are to describe their every move to their partner who will try to draw the identical picture from the description. The lead students may not tell their partners what they are drawing (i.e. "I am drawing a house") but they may tell them positions (top, bottom, etc.), directions (left, right, etc.) and shapes (i.e. "Starting in the middle at the top of the page, I am drawing a diagonal line to the right side about three inches long").
- When the game is finished, discuss the following questions:
  1. What communication skills did you need to do this activity successfully?
  2. What role was easiest, to be the explainer or the listener?
  3. In prayer what is easier, to ask God for what you want or to listen to what God wants for you?

𝕀N THE WORD (25-30 MINUTES)

A CONVERSATION WITH THE COMMANDER
- Divide students into groups of three or four.
- Give each student a copy of "In the Word" on pages 138-141 and a pen or pencil, or dis-

---- Fold ----

play a copy using an overhead projector.
- Have students complete the Bible study.

1. Communication is the key that resolves many battles in life. This is also true in the battles that believers fight every-day. In Ephesians 6:18, what does Paul tell believers to do after they have put on the full armor of God?

2. How does prayer keep believers alert?

3. What must we be alert for?

PRAYER THAT WINS
1. Turn to Matthew 16:13-19 and eavesdrop on a conversation between Jesus, Simon Peter and the rest of the disciples. Jesus asks the question "Who do people say the Son of Man is?" What is their response in verse 14?

2. Now Jesus turns up the heat by directing the next question toward them. Jesus asks "But what about you?...Who do you say I am?" (v. 15). Who is the first to answer the question?

3. If Peter had been off doing something else, would he have been able to answer Jesus?

COMPONENT ONE: PRAY CONSISTENTLY.
1. What does James 4:2,3 say are the two reasons we don't receive more answers from God?

2. What are some reasons why people don't pray consistently?

3. What are some examples of selfish prayers?

4. Peter received a response from Christ because he made the time to spend with Him. What is the longest that you have consistently prayed for something before receiving an answer?

| a. one week | b. one month | c. three months |
| d. six months | e. one year | f. even longer |

COMPONENT TWO: PRAY BELIEVING GOD CAN.
1. In Matthew 16:16, what is Peter's response to Jesus' question?

2. Here Peter shows us the second component of prayer that is victorious. What does James 1:5,6 say Christians must do and not do to win with prayer?

3. James says "he who doubts is like a wave of the sea, blown and tossed by the wind" (v.6). What should that person expect to receive from God and why (v. 7)?

CONSTANT CONTACT WITH THE COMMANDER-IN-CHIEF

WARM UP

IF I WERE GOD...

List 10 things you would do differently if you were God today.

1. If I were God, I would... ....
....

2. If I were God, I would... ....
....

3. If I were God, I would... ....
....

4. If I were God, I would... ....
....

5. If I were God, I would... ....
....

6. If I were God, I would... ....
....

7. If I were God, I would... ....
....

8. If I were God, I would... ....
....

9. If I were God, I would... ....
....

10. If I were God, I would... ....
....

CONSTANT
CONTACT WITH THE
COMMANDER-IN-
CHIEF

PUTTING ON GOD'S ARMOR

IN THE WORD

A CONVERSATION WITH THE COMMANDER

1. Communication is the key that resolves many battles in life. This is also true in the battles that believers fight every day. In Ephesians 6:18, what does Paul tell believers to do after they have put on the full armor of God?

....

....

2. How does prayer keep believers alert?

....

....

3. What must we be alert for?

....

....

Prayer that Wins

1. Turn to Matthew 16:13-19 and eavesdrop on a conversation between Jesus, Simon Peter and the rest of the disciples. Jesus asks the question "Who do people say the Son of Man is?" What is their response in verse 14?

....

....

2. Now Jesus turns up the heat by directing the next question toward them. Jesus asks "But what about you?...Who do you say I am?" (v. 15). Who is the first to answer the question?

....

....

3. If Peter had been off doing something else, would he have been able to answer Jesus?

....

....

Component One: Pray Consistently.

Peter came on time! If he had been five minutes late or hadn't come at all, he would have had an "I-should-have-been-there" experience.

1. What does James 4:2,3 say are the two reasons we don't receive more answers from God?

....

....

2. What are some reasons why people don't pray consistently?

....

....

CONSTANT
CONTACT WITH THE
COMMANDER-IN-
CHIEF

IN THE WORD

3. What are some examples of selfish prayers?

4. Peter received a response from Christ because he made the time to spend with Him. What is the longest that you have consistently prayed for something before receiving an answer?

a. one week   b. one month   c. three months

d. six months   e. one year   f. even longer

Component Two: Pray Believing God Can.

1. In Matthew 16:16, what is Peter's response to Jesus' question?

2. Here Peter shows us the second component of prayer that is victorious. What does James 1:5,6 say Christians must do and not do to win with prayer?

3. James says "he who doubts is like a wave of the sea, blown and tossed by the wind" (v. 6). What should that person expect to receive from God and why (v. 7)?

Take the Belief or Doubt Challenge

First take this piece of paper representing doubt—which is a feeling—and place it in your hands. Blow on it as hard as you can. What happens? This paper is like the person who feels doubt in God, leading him or her to believe that God can't!

Now take something solid and kind of heavy (like keys, a book or a rock). Place the solid object in the palm of your hand and blow. What happens to it? This object represents the person who chooses to believe that God can!

4. Peter takes the belief-or-doubt challenge in Matthew 14:22-33. What happens to Peter that brings him to confidently say "truly you are the Son of God" in Matthew 14:33?

Component Three: Pray Specifically.

1. In Matthew 14:29, Jesus asks Peter to step out of the boat and walk on the water. In verse 28, Peter demonstrates the third component of prayer—to pray specifically for what you need. Even though this verse is not stated in the form of a question, what was Peter specifically asking Jesus to reveal to him?

IN THE WORD

2. What is Jesus' immediate response?

....

....

3. What does James 4:2 say is the reason we don't have answers to our prayers?

....

....

Component Four: Pray Expecting to Hear God's Voice.

1. After asking God specifically for something, most Christians get up from praying and walk out thinking: It is all over. I've done my part. What does Matthew 16:17 say that points to Component Four of victorious prayer? In other words, how did Peter know the answer to Jesus' question (v. 17)?

....

....

2. Peter listened for Christ's response. So many Christians leave their prayer time before the Lord has a chance to respond to their questions. What are the five specific statements that Jesus makes in His response to Peter in Matthew 16:17-19.

    a. The blessing: ....

....

    b. A confirmation that Peter had heard God correctly: ....

....

    c. A name change: ....

....

    d. A life purpose: ....

....

    e. The equipment to live out that purpose: ....

....

SO WHAT?

A Prayer Plan

The best way to pray to win is to practice. Here is a simple structure you can use to prepare yourself for a winning conversation with God. The structure is based on Philippians 4:4-7. It can be done verbally, silently or in a prayer journal. It is much easier to remember the thoughts and verses you may hear while listening when you write them down in a journal or on a note

pad. The greatest battles are won in prayer. Take the time to practice step-by-step as a group using the structure below.

Step One: **P**raise God for Who He is.

> "Rejoice in the Lord always. I will say it again: Rejoice!" (Philippians 4:4).

Complete the sentence: Dear God I praise You for being... ....

....

Step Two: **R**epent humbly and honestly for your sins.

> "Let your gentleness be evident to all. The Lord is near. Do not be anxious about anything" (Philippians 4:5,6).

Complete the sentence: Dear God, please forgive me for... ....

....

Step Three: **A**ppreciate God for what He has done and is doing in your life.

> "But in everything, by prayer and petition, with thanksgiving"
> (Philippians 4:6).

Complete the sentence: Dear God, thank You for... ....

....

Step Four: **Y**ou ask specifically, believing God can.

> "Present your requests to God" (Philippians 4:6).

Complete the sentence: Dear God, I ask You... ....

....

Step Five: **E**xpect to hear God's voice.

> "And the peace of God, which transcends all understanding" (Philippians 4:7).

Complete the sentence: Dear God, I am listening (write down any thoughts, impressions, verses or reminders that come into your head). ....

....

Step Six: **R**eceive and write it down to test it against God's written word.

> "Will guard your hearts and your minds in Christ Jesus" (Philippians 4:7).
> "Test everything" (1 Thessalonians 5:21).

Complete the sentence: Dear God, I hear you saying... ....

....

CONSTANT CONTACT WITH THE COMMANDER-IN-CHIEF

Things to Think About

1. What are two ways you have seen prayer work in your life or in the life of someone you know.

....

....

....

2. What is one thing that you would ask God to do for you right now if He were standing in the room?

....

....

....

3. What keeps you from asking Him everyday in prayer to meet your needs and/or for His help?

....

....

....

  142

Listening for God's Voice

1. Share a time when you saw God answer your prayer or someone else's prayer in a dramatic way.

2. Have you ever heard God speak to you? Explain.

3. How did you know it was His voice?

4. Read Joshua 1:1. Who spoke to Joshua?

5. Joshua gets an earful in verses 2-9. What does God promise Joshua in verse 9?

6. Why do you think God gave Joshua these instructions and encouragements?

7. God promises to give us strength when we are weak, answers when we are confused, courage when we are afraid and hope when we feel defeated. What is one issue or concern about which you feel you need some answers or encouragement?

James 1:5,6 says "If any of you lacks wisdom, he should ask God, who gives generously to all without finding fault, and it will be given to him. But when he asks, he must believe and not doubt."

Take some time in prayer together asking God for what you need, believing that He will faithfully give it to you at the right time.

Session 12 "Constant Contact with the Commander-in-Chief" Date

Add a New Member to Your Youth Staff.

Jim Burns is president of the National Institute of Youth Ministry.

Meet Jim Burns. He won't play guitar and he doesn't do windows, but he will take care of your programming needs. That's because his new curriculum, **YouthBuilders Group Bible Studies,** is a comprehensive program designed to take your group through their high school years. (If you have junior high kids in your group, **YouthBuilders** works for them too.)

For less than $6 a month, you'll get Jim Burns' special recipe of high-involvement, discussion-oriented, Bible-centered studies. It's the next generation of Bible curriculum for youth—and with Jim on your staff, you'll be free to spend more time one-on-one with the kids in your group.

Here are some of Youth-Builders' hottest features:

- Reproducible pages—one book fits your whole group
- Wide appeal—big groups, small groups—even adjusts to combine junior high/high school groups
- Hits home—special section to involve parents with every session of the study
- Interactive Bible discovery—geared to help young people find answers themselves
- Cheat sheets—a Bible *Tuck-In*™ with all the session information on a single page
- Flexible format—perfect for Sunday mornings, midweek youth meetings, or camps and retreats
- Three studies in one—each study has three four-session modules that examine critical life choices.

   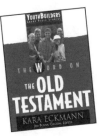 

12 Books in the Series!

The Word on Sex, Drugs & Rock 'N' Roll
ISBN 08307.16424 $16.99

The Word on Prayer and the Devotional Life
ISBN 08307.16432 $16.99

The Word on the Basics of Christianity
ISBN 08307.16440 $16.99

The Word on Being a Leader, Serving Others & Sharing Your Faith
ISBN 08307.16459 $16.99

The Word on Helping Friends in Crisis
ISBN 08307.16467 $16.99

The Word on the Life of Jesus
ISBN 08307.16475 $16.99

The Word on Finding and Using Your Spiritual Gifts
ISBN 08307.17897 $16.99

The Word on the Sermon on the Mount
ISBN 08307.17234 $16.99

The Word on Spiritual Warfare
ISBN 08307.17242 $16.99

The Word on the New Testament
ISBN 08307.17250 $16.99

The Word on the Old Testament
ISBN 08307.17269 $16.99

The Word on Family
ISBN 08307.17277 $16.99

More Great Resources from Jim Burns

Drugproof Your Kids
Stephen Arterburn and Jim Burns

Solid biblical principles are combined with the most effective prevention and intervention techniques to give parents a guide they can trust.
ISBN 08307.17714 $10.99

Drugproof Your Kids Video
A 90-minute seminar featuring Stephen Arterburn and Jim Burns. Includes a reproducible syllabus.
SPCN 85116.00876 $19.99

Parenting Teens Positively
Video *Featuring Jim Burns*

Understand the forces shaping the world of a teenager and what you can do to be a positive influence. This powerful message of hope is for anyone working with—or living with—youth. Includes reproducible syllabus. UPC 607135.000655 $29.99

Surviving Adolescence
Jim Burns

Jim Burns helps teens—and their parents—negotiate the path from adolescence to adulthood with real-life stories that show how to make it through the teen years in one piece. ISBN 08307.20650 $9.99

For these and more great resources and to learn about NIYM's leadership training, call **1-800-397-9725.**

Gospel Light

FRESH IDEAS

RESOURCES FOR YOUTH WORKERS

Jim Burns, General Editor

Turn your youth group meetings into dynamic, exciting events that kids look forward to attending week after week! Supercharge your messages, grab their attention with your activities and connect with kids the first time and every time with these great resources. Just try to keep these books on the shelf!

ILLUSTRATIONS, STORIES AND QUOTES TO HANG YOUR MESSAGE ON

Few things get your point across faster or with greater impact than a memorable story with a twist. Grab your teens' attention by talking with your mouth full of unforgettable stories.
Manual, ISBN 08307.18834 $16.99

CASE STUDIES, TALK SHEETS AND DISCUSSION STARTERS

Teens learn best when they talk—not when you talk at them. A discussion allowing youth to discover the truth for themselves, with your guidance, is a powerful experience that will stay with them for a lifetime.
Manual, ISBN 08307.18842 $16.99

GAMES, CROWDBREAKERS AND COMMUNITY BUILDERS

Dozens of innovative, youth-group-tested ideas for fun and original crowdbreakers, as well as successful plans and trips for building a sense of community in your group.
Manual, ISBN 08307.18818 $16.99

More Resources for Youth Workers, Parents & Students

Steering Them Straight
Stephen Arterburn & Jim Burns

Parents can find understanding as well as practical tools to deal with crisis situations. Includes guidelines that will help any family prevent problems before they develop.
UPC 156179.4066 $10.99

The Youth Builder
Jim Burns

This Gold Medallion Award winner provides you with proven methods, specific recommendations and hands-on examples of handling and understanding the problems and challenges of youth ministry.
ISBN 089081.1576. $16.95

Spirit Wings
Jim Burns

In the language of today's teens, these 84 short devotionals will encourage youth to build a stronger and more intimate relationship with God.
ISBN 08928.37837 $10.95

Radical Love
Book & Video, Jim Burns

In *Radical Love* kids discover why it's best to wait on God's timing, how to say no when their bodies say yes and how to find forgiveness for past mistakes.
Paperback, ISBN 08307.17935 $9.99
VHS Video, SPCN 85116.00922 $19.99

90 Days Through the New Testament
Jim Burns

A growth experience through the New Testament that lays the foundation for developing a daily time with God.
ISBN 08307.14561 $9.99

Getting in Touch with God
Jim Burns

Develop a consistent and disciplined time with God in the midst of hectic schedules as Jim Burns shares with you inspiring devotional readings to deepen your love of God.
ISBN 08908.15208 $2.95

Radical Christianity
Book & Video, Jim Burns

Radical Christianity is a proven plan to help youth live a life that's worth living and make a difference in their world.
Paperback, ISBN 08307.17927 $9.99
VHS Video, SPCN 85116.01082 $19.99

The Youth Worker's Book of Case Studies
Jim Burns

Fifty-two true stories with discussion questions to add interest to Bible studies.
ISBN 08307.15827 $12.99

What in the world is *NIYM*?

A.) The Neurotically Inclined Yo-Yo Masters
B.) The Neatest Incidental Yearbook Mystery
C.) The Natural Ignition Yields of Marshmallows
D.) The National Institute of Youth Ministry

If you deliberately picked A, B, or C you're the reason Jim Burns started NIYM! If you picked D, you can go to the next page. In any case, you could learn more about NIYM. Here are some IQ score-raisers:

Jim Burns started NIYM to:
• Meet the growing needs of training and equipping youth workers and parents
• Develop excellent resources and events for young people—in the U.S. and internationally
• Empower young people and their families to make wise decisions and experience a vital Christian lifestyle.

NIYM can make a difference in your life and enhance your youth work skills through these special events:

Institutes—These consist of week-long, in-depth small-group training sessions for youth workers.

Trainer of Trainees—NIYM will train you to train others. You can use this training with your volunteers, parents and denominational events. You can go through the certification process and become an official NIYM associate. (No, you don't get a badge or decoder ring).

International Training—Join NIYM associates to bring youth ministry to kids and adults around the world. (You'll learn meanings to universal words like "yo!" and "hey!')

Custom Training—These are special training events for denominational groups, churches, networks, colleges and seminaries.

Parent Forums—We'll come to your church or community with two incredible hours of learning, interaction and fellowship. It'll be fun finding out who makes your kids tick!

Youth Events—Dynamic speakers, interaction and drama bring a powerful message to kids through a fun and fast-paced day. Our youth events include: This Side Up, Radical Respect, Surviving Adolescence and Peer Leadership.

For brain food or a free information packet about the National Institute of Youth Ministry, write to:

NIYM

P.O. Box 297 • San Juan Capistrano, CA 92675
Tel: (949) 487-0217 • Fax: (949) 487-1758 • Info@niym.org

ACTIONS *speak* LOUDER WITH WORDS

...and Roger's got a milliOn of theM.

FOR NEARLY 15 YEARS COMEDIC COMMUNICATOR ROGER ROYSTER HAS REACHED INTO HIS BAG OF TRICKS USING COMEDY, DRAMA, VISUALS, AND MUSIC TO GIVE HIS LISTENERS LEARNING EXPERIENCES THAT ARE EASY TO UNDERSTAND AND HARD TO FORGET. IN A WORLD WITH TOO MANY OPTIONS AND TOO FEW ANSWERS, PEOPLE NEED SOMEONE WILLING TO HELP THEM UNDERSTAND THE TRUTH. ROGER'S UNIQUE STYLE OF COMMUNICATION HAS MADE HIM A POPULAR SPEAKER IN SCHOOLS, CHURCHES, YOUTH GROUPS AND CAMP SETTINGS ACROSS THE NATION. HIS HONEST AND ENERGETIC HUMOR POWERFULLY COMMUNICATES TRUTH TO PEOPLE WITH EARS TO HEAR. ROGER IS PRESENTLY ADOLESCENT SERVICES CHAPLAIN FOR MINIRTH MEIER NEW LIFE TREATMENT CLINIC IN ORANGE COUNTY CALIFORNIA, ON STAFF WITH THE NATIONAL INSTITUTE OF YOUTH MINISTRY, AND IS DIRECTOR OF WACKY WORLD COMMUNICATIONS, AN ORGANIZATION DEDICATED TO BEING A VOICE OF HOPE, ENCOURAGEMENT AND EDUCATION TO A WORLD GONE "WACKY."

"Roger is a very gifted communicator and a very funny comedian. He has the ability and integrity to effectively communicate God's message to parents and teens in the 90's."
–Jim Burns, President, National Institute of Youth Ministry

"He is the best in his field..."
–Jane Borba, Children's Director, Yorba Linda Friends

"The finest speaker I have ever heard.."
–Charlotte Royster, Roger's Mom

For information and booking call:

714·638·2377
714·498·4418

E-Mail Address: Wacky RR @AOL

or write:

Roger Royster
Wacky World Communications
P.O. Box 2121
Garden Grove, CA 92640